AYATOLLAH
RUHOLLAH
KHOMEINI

SPIRITUAL LEADERS AND THINKERS

MARY BAKER EDDY

MOHANDAS GANDHI

AYATOLLAH RUHOLLAH KHOMEINI

MARTIN LUTHER

AIMEE SEMPLE McPHERSON

THOMAS MERTON

DALAI LAMA (TENZIN GYATSO)

SPIRITUAL
LEADERS AND
THINKERS

AYATOLLAH RUHOLLAH KHOMEINI

Daniel E. Harmon

Introductory Essay by
Martin E. Marty, Professor Emeritus
University of Chicago Divinity School

CHELSEA HOUSE
PUBLISHERS
A Haights Cross Communications Company

Philadelphia

CHELSEA HOUSE PUBLISHERS

VP, NEW PRODUCT DEVELOPMENT   Sally Cheney
DIRECTOR OF PRODUCTION   Kim Shinners
CREATIVE MANAGER   Takeshi Takahashi
MANUFACTURING MANAGER   Diann Grasse

Staff for AYATOLLAH RUHOLLAH KHOMEINI

EXECUTIVE EDITOR   Lee Marcott
SENIOR EDITOR   Tara Koellhoffer
PRODUCTION EDITOR   Megan Emery
ASSOCIATE PHOTO EDITOR   Noelle Nardone
SERIES AND COVER DESIGNER   Keith Trego
LAYOUT   21st Century Publishing and Communications, Inc.

A Haights Cross Communications ◀▐▬ Company

www.chelseahouse.com

First Printing

9 8 7 6 5 4 3 2 1

Library of Congress Cataloging-in-Publication Data

Harmon, Daniel E.
    Ayatollah Ruhollah Khomeini/Daniel E. Harmon.
       p. cm.—(Spiritual leaders and thinkers)
Includes bibliographical references.
    ISBN 0-7910-7865-5
    1. Khomeini, Ruhollah—Juvenile literature. 2. Heads of state—Iran—
Biography—Juvenile literature. 3. Iran—History—1979-1997—Juvenile
literature. I. Title. II. Series.
DS318.84.K48H37 2004
955.05'42'092—dc22

                                                              2004002723

CONTENTS

Foreword

Why become acquainted with notable people when making efforts to understand the religions of the world?

Most of the faith communities number hundreds of millions of people. What can attention paid to one tell about more, if not most, to say nothing of *all*, their adherents? Here is why:

The people in this series are exemplars. If you permit me to take a little detour through medieval dictionaries, their role will become clear.

In medieval lexicons, the word *exemplum* regularly showed up with a peculiar definition. No one needs to know Latin to see that it relates to "example" and "exemplary." But back then, *exemplum* could mean something very special.

That "ex-" at the beginning of such words signals "taking out" or "cutting out" something or other. Think of to "excise" something, which is to snip it out. So, in the more interesting dictionaries, an *exemplum* was referred to as "a clearing in the woods," something cut out of the forests.

These religious figures are *exempla*, figurative clearings in the woods of life. These clearings and these people perform three functions:

First, they define. You can be lost in the darkness, walking under the leafy canopy, above the undergrowth, plotless in the pathless forest. Then you come to a clearing. It defines with a sharp line: there, the woods end; here, the open space begins.

Great religious figures are often stumblers in the dark woods.

We see them emerging in the bright light of the clearing, blinking, admitting that they had often been lost in the mysteries of existence, tangled up with the questions that plague us all, wandering without definition. Then they discover the clearing, and, having done so, they point our way to it. We then learn more of who we are and where we are. Then we can set our own direction.

Second, the *exemplum*, the clearing in the woods of life, makes possible a brighter vision. Great religious pioneers in every case experience illumination and then they reflect their light into the hearts and minds of others. In Buddhism, a key word is *enlightenment*. In the Bible, "the people who walked in darkness have seen a great light." They see it because their prophets or savior brought them to the sun in the clearing.

Finally, when you picture a clearing in the woods, an *exemplum*, you are likely to see it as a place of cultivation. Whether in the Black Forest of Germany, on the American frontier, or in the rain forests of Brazil, the clearing is the place where, with light and civilization, residents can cultivate, can produce culture. As an American moviegoer, my mind's eye remembers cinematic scenes of frontier days and places that pioneers hacked out of the woods. There, they removed stones, planted, built a cabin, made love and produced families, smoked their meat, hung out laundered clothes, and read books. All that can happen in clearings.

In the case of these religious figures, planting and cultivating and harvesting are tasks in which they set an example and then inspire or ask us to follow. Most of us would not have the faintest idea how to find or be found by God, to nurture the Holy Spirit, to create a philosophy of life without guidance. It is not likely that most of us would be satisfied with our search if we only consulted books of dogma or philosophy, though such may come to have their place in the clearing.

Philosopher Søren Kierkegaard properly pointed out that you cannot learn to swim by being suspended from the ceiling on a belt and reading a "How To" book on swimming. You learn because a parent or an instructor plunges you into water, supports you when necessary, teaches you breathing and motion, and then releases you to swim on your own.

Kierkegaard was not criticizing the use of books. I certainly have nothing against books. If I did, I would not be commending this series to you, as I am doing here. For guidance and courage in the spiritual quest, or—and this is by no means unimportant!—in intellectual pursuits, involving efforts to understand the paths others have taken, there seems to be no better way than to follow a fellow mortal, but a man or woman of genius, depth, and daring. We "see" them through books like these.

Exemplars come in very different styles and forms. They bring differing kinds of illumination, and then suggest or describe diverse patterns of action to those who join them. In the case of the present series, it is possible for someone to repudiate or disagree with *all* the religious leaders in this series. It is possible also to be nonreligious and antireligious and therefore to disregard the truth claims of all of them. It is more difficult, however, to ignore them. Atheists, agnostics, adherents, believers, and fanatics alike live in cultures that are different for the presence of these people. "Leaders and thinkers" they may be, but most of us do best to appraise their thought in the context of the lives they lead or have led.

If it is possible to reject them all, it is impossible to affirm everything that all of them were about. They disagree with each other, often in basic ways. Sometimes they develop their positions and ways of thinking by separating themselves from all the others. If they met each other, they would likely judge each other cruelly. Yet the lives of each and all of them make a contribution to the intellectual and spiritual quests of those who go in ways other than theirs. There are tens of thousands of religions in the world, and millions of faith communities. Every one of them has been shaped by founders and interpreters, agents of change and prophets of doom or promise. It may seem arbitrary to walk down a bookshelf and let a finger fall on one or another, almost accidentally. This series may certainly look arbitrary in this way. Why precisely the choice of these exemplars?

In some cases, it is clear that the publishers have chosen someone who has a constituency. Many of the world's 54 million Lutherans may be curious about where they got their name, who the man Martin Luther was. Others are members of a community but choose isolation: The hermit monk Thomas Merton is typical. Still others are exiled and achieve their work far from the clearing in which they grew up; here the Dalai Lama is representative. Quite a number of the selected leaders had been made unwelcome, or felt unwelcome in the clearings, in their own childhoods and youth. This reality has almost always been the case with women like Mary Baker Eddy or Aimee Semple McPherson. Some are extremely controversial: Ayatollah Ruhollah Khomeini stands out. Yet to read of this life and thought as one can in this series will be illuminating in much of the world of conflict today.

Reading of religious leaders can be a defensive act: Study the lives of certain ones among them and you can ward off spiritual—and sometimes even militant—assaults by people who follow them. Reading and learning can be a personally positive act: Most of these figures led lives that we can indeed call exemplary. Such lives can throw light on communities of people who are in no way tempted to follow them. I am not likely to be drawn to the hermit life, will not give up my allegiance to medical doctors, or be successfully nonviolent. Yet Thomas Merton reaches me and many non-Catholics in our communities; Mary Baker Eddy reminds others that there are more ways than one to approach healing; Mohandas Gandhi stings the conscience of people in cultures like ours where resorting to violence is too frequent, too easy.

Finally, reading these lives tells something about how history is made by imperfect beings. None of these subjects is a god, though some of them claimed that they had special access to the divine, or that they were like windows that provided for illumination to that which is eternal. Most of their stories began with inauspicious childhoods. Sometimes they were victimized, by parents or by leaders of religions from which they later broke.

Some of them were unpleasant and abrasive. They could be ungracious toward those who were near them and impatient with laggards. If their lives were symbolic clearings, places for light, many of them also knew clouds and shadows and the fall of night. How they met the challenges of life and led others to face them is central to the plot of all of them.

I have often used a rather unexciting concept to describe what I look for in books: *interestingness*. The authors of these books, one might say, had it easy, because the characters they treat are themselves so interesting. But the authors also had to be interesting and responsible. If, as they wrote, they would have dulled the personalities of their bright characters, that would have been a flaw as marring as if they had treated their subjects without combining fairness and criticism, affection and distance. To my eye, and I hope in yours, they take us to spiritual and intellectual clearings that are so needed in our dark times.

Martin E. Marty
The University of Chicago

1

An Astonishing Transition in Power

M uhammad Reza Shah Pahlavi, ruler of Iran, had a fortune withdrawn from royal bank accounts in early 1979. On the afternoon of January 16, dressed smartly in a three-piece suit, he boarded the royal jet with his wife and entourage at the Tehran airport. An avid pilot, the shah himself settled at the controls and took flight. The destination: Egypt—one of the few countries in the world where he knew he would find a welcome. Soon after they were airborne, the shah turned the plane over to his staff pilot and went to his personal quarters. Perhaps he retreated there to rest. Perhaps he went to brood. Or perhaps to weep.

It had been announced that the shah and his family were taking a vacation, but the reality was that the Pahlavis would never return. The shah knew he was seeing the last of his homeland as his plane rose and banked above the capital city. He carried among his valuables a box of Iranian soil, a melancholy symbol of an ousted leader's failed vision.

Masses of Iranians who celebrated his departure also knew the shah was gone for good. They knew a very different leader would soon arrive to replace him, and this made them extremely happy. News that the shah's plane had taken off was broadcast immediately over the radio. Joyful shouting, singing, dancing, and horn blowing rose to the skies behind him.

Two weeks later, an inbound Air France jet taxied to a halt at the Tehran airport. From it, assisted carefully by the flight crew, emerged a seventy-eight-year-old man. He was tall and bearded, with a dark, chilling glare of a countenance born of years of anger directed toward Shah Pahlavi's regime. In a matter of days, this man would dramatically alter the history of an ancient land and deal the Western world a stunning jolt. He was Ayatollah Sayyid Ruhollah Musavi Khomeini, an Iranian religious leader who had been exiled for his radical activities since the early 1960s. Khomeini was accompanied by some fifty aides and close associates, as well as more than one hundred journalists who had come to cover a revolution in the making.

To those in power, the ayatollah's return to Iran was more than a little alarming. His hysterical reception, led by the nation's student generation, horrified them. An estimated 2 to 3 million Iranians swarmed the streets, creating such a horde of enthusiastic chaos that the ayatollah had to be transported from the airport by helicopter.

Ayatollah Khomeini was in some ways a mystery figure—not just to outsiders who were riveted by the unfolding news from the Middle East, but to his own people. He had become the most respected, idolized Iranian in the world during the fifteen years when he wasn't even in the country. From exile, he had relentlessly preached revolution. For years, his sermons had been smuggled into Iran and distributed among mushrooming legions of admirers. More recently, his message had been broadcast worldwide by mainline media. Most Iranians had come to agree with his accusations of corruption within the shah's regime and had clamored for Khomeini to return from exile and bring justice to their land. Yet few of them had ever met the man behind the message. Those who had met Khomeini found him glowering and aloof, not given to courteous greetings or to weighing the opinions of others.

Most of his people believed in his general vision: a new government and society controlled by Islam. But they had little idea how it would develop. A decade later, when he died, he would leave behind a population that was growing increasingly unhappy with the system he created.

When he returned to his homeland that winter, however, Khomeini immediately commanded the homage—the very spirit—of Iranians. He immediately became the unquestioned force behind the Iranian government.

How had this small-town, childhood orphan risen to such power?

In Iranian universities, discontented students during the 1960s became politically active in opposing the shah's regime. Most notable among their leaders was Khomeini. An outspoken Shiite teacher (Shiism is a branch of Islam), he lost his position and, eventually, his citizenship. Ordered out of Iran, he continued to write and tape messages demanding the overthrow of the shah. His followers in Iran, growing in number, devoured his messages. They declared themselves loyal to him and eagerly awaited his return.

Throughout this period of exile, Khomeini was virtually unknown outside the region. Even to people in other Middle Eastern countries, he was at most an obscure Muslim leader. It is difficult to find a mention of his name in books on Iranian history and affairs published before 1979, the year he burst into the spotlight of world news.

Although he became Iran's foremost religious leader—never its official head of government—Khomeini is remembered as one of the most famous and forceful figures in Middle East politics. He has been ranked with leaders such as Israel's Prime Minister Menachem Begin, Jordan's King Hussein I, Egypt's President Anwar el-Sadat, and Libya's Colonel Muammar al-Qaddafi.

The story of Ayatollah Ruhollah Khomeini is a story of Shiite Islam's evolving impact on the modern world, for he became Shiism's most eminent speaker. And it is a story of Khomeini's long-time antagonist, Shah Pahlavi. Khomeini's career as a revolutionary was built entirely on his opposition to the Pahlavi government. The Iranian people saw in these two men rival characters of epic proportions: Pahlavi an unjust, corrupt tyrant and Khomeini their avenger and guiding light.

Essentially, though, the story of Ayatollah Khomeini is the story of the Iranian Revolution. Of the many voices raised to condemn the Pahlavi regime during the 1960s and 1970s, Khomeini's commanded the masses. When he attained his life-long objective after years of protest from exile, Iranians gave him complete authority to forge whatever new government he wished. His new government has been, by every account, a force to be reckoned with, not only in the Middle East but worldwide. Even now, fifteen years after his death, life and government in Iran are based largely on the stern vision of Ayatollah Khomeini.

2

The "Land Between East and West"

Until the revolution of 1979, most Westerners viewed Iran with dreamy curiosity. The name brought to mind exotic, not chaotic, images. The West did not see a dangerously discontent people, but a land with a romantic history. Its leader, the shah, was a reliable American ally—a good friend to have in a petroleum-rich but sometimes turbulent part of the world.

Iran's ancient legacy, true enough, is filled with splendor and mystique. Probed deeply by archaeologists, the country has much to tell about one of the world's earliest known civilizations. Bronze Age settlements were established there around 4000 B.C. At Hasanlu, scientists have found walls and other remnants of towns believed to date to the biblical age of Abraham. Unearthed skeletons in cringing postures, almost three thousand years old, suggest massive, sudden destruction. It was a place of violence and uncertainty even in tribal times.

Later, what is now Iran was the center of the great Persian Empire. At its height, Persia spread from present-day Pakistan, Afghanistan, and Turkmenistan in the east to Egypt and the southern fringe of Europe in the west. Appropriately, Persia was called "the land between East and West."

Persia first became a dominant kingdom during the sixth and fifth centuries B.C. under the reigns of Cyrus the Great, Darius I, and Darius's son Xerxes. This was a glorious period of military supremacy. After defeating the legendary Babylonians in 540 B.C., Cyrus proclaimed himself "king of the universe." Later, Xerxes invaded Greece with a force believed to have been almost 2 million strong.

Persia was a kingdom of incalculable wealth, a source of precious metals and jewels. King Darius established a sprawling city at Persepolis ("City of Persia"). Many of Persepolis's rows of stone columns—100 columns supported the roof of the throne room alone—have weathered the ages to the present day. Subjects from throughout the kingdom were required to pay tribute to the king by bringing him minerals and jewels, carpets, silk, and other valuables. Artisans recorded the empire's might in sculptures and stone carvings. They left such depictions as court visitors bowing before Darius on his throne, subjects parading with treasures to the palace, and a conquered invader shackled and kneeling before his Persian master.

Defeated by Alexander the Great of Macedon in 331 B.C., Persia fell under the governance of several ruling dynasties for several hundred years. But a "new Persia" emerged in

PERSIA'S FABLED RULERS

The Pahlavi shahs of the twentieth century wanted to make Iran an industrialized, "Westernized" leader of the Middle East while also glorifying its 2,500-year history. They looked proudly to the glorious Persia of Cyrus the Great and his successors.

Cyrus, who rose to power in 558 B.C., is perhaps most renowned in history for his conquest of the powerful Babylonian Empire. Not merely a military commander of great ingenuity, he was also a sensitive ruler. He made little attempt to change the defeated people who fell under his control, but instead permitted them to live much as they had lived before. To a high degree, they could govern themselves, speak their familiar languages, and continue their traditional religious practices. Such a policy was as shrewd as it was generous; by giving his conquests basically free rein, he had little fear of uprisings.

Cyrus appreciated the finer things in life—not just jewels and economic wealth, but natural beauty. His capital at Pasargadae featured a spectacular garden of flowers, trees, and pools.

King Darius I, who ascended to the throne several years after Cyrus's death, left an even grander legacy: the holy city of Persepolis. Its ruins tell of magnificent palaces and temples. But Persepolis is noted for its practical engineering as well as for its stone columns, carvings, and other splendor. It had, for example, an advanced water and sewer system. Darius meanwhile oversaw the building of the Royal Highway, a system of paved, guarded roads that provided easy and safe passage for caravan traders.

The Pahlavis who came to power much later shared these great kings' appreciation of grandeur, sophistication, and national improvements. What they woefully lacked was the savvy to lead their people effectively while dealing with the outside world. This shortcoming would bring about their ruin.

A.D. 224 and spread. It included parts of what are now Turkey and India—a vast domain. Persia reached its height in the early seventh century A.D., when it bounded the Black Sea to the north.

Soon afterward, Persia was conquered by Arab invaders. They made their capital in what is now Baghdad, an ancient city on the Tigris River that today is the capital of Iraq. The Arab ruler, called a *caliph*, summoned master artisans—silversmiths, woodcrafters, sculptors, glassmakers—and architects from across the Arab domain to develop Baghdad into one of the most magnificent centers of power the world has ever known. Baghdad assumed a round shape, two miles in diameter. The royal palace at its center was built of marble, topped with a dome of gold to command the awe of citizens and visitors alike. Inside were the most intricate carpets, inlay, and works of art.

Visitors from near and far flocked to the capital. Baghdad became a center of caravan trade for the entire region. Scholars, artists, and astronomers were drawn to it. The caliphs brought musicians, poets, and storytellers to entertain at court. Variations of some of their handed-down tales eventually were compiled and published in France: *The Thousand Nights and a Night* is famous today as *The Arabian Nights*. Baghdad became known as a grand city of enlightenment. To the rest of the world, a mention of Persia or Arabia evoked delighted visions of exotic music and dance, genies in bottles, jolly slaves and bakers in billowy trousers, dragon slayers, treasure-laden camel caravans arriving via the Silk Route from distant China, black-mustachioed cavalrymen brandishing scimitars, stellar night canopies above enchanting city skylines of domes and minarets, and harems of beautiful young women.

But the Arabs introduced something quite different and far more enduring than a kingdom of opulence. A new form of religion, Islam, replaced that of the Persian prophet Zoroaster. In time, the caliph became regarded as Islam's spiritual leader.

While different groups—Seljuks, Mongols, and Turkomans—would rule the region over a period of more than a thousand years, Islam would remain constant.

Islam was founded in the 600s by a man who, as an orphaned youth, had been a lowly shepherd. His name was Muhammad ibn Abdullah. He later would be known as the prophet Muhammad. His system of belief, based on a dream, would become a major influence on modern Middle Eastern religion and politics. It would be the religion of Ayatollah Khomeini and would serve as the basis for Iran's revolution more than a thousand years later.

MUHAMMAD'S ANGELIC VISIONS

The prophet Muhammad, founder of Islam, was born to a tribe of traders in Mecca, a city now located in Saudi Arabia. Raised by an uncle, he grew to be a caravan merchant and traveled great distances across the Arabian deserts. But it was not his trading that made him wealthy; it was his marriage to a well-off widow named Khadijah. With her, he lived a comfortable, ordinary life until he reached middle age.

At that time, he began taking moody sojourns into the mountains near Mecca. On one of these retreats, on what Muslims call the Night of Power, Muhammad felt called to be a prophet. He understood that he was to recite to the citizens of Mecca a sequence of messages he received from God through Gabriel, the archangel. From then until the end of his life, Muhammad regularly proclaimed the divine revelations that eventually would become the Qur'an, or Koran. They teach that Allah, the only God, is a God of compassion. They warn against idolatry and tell of a coming judgment day.

His teachings proved to be not altogether popular, for many people of Mecca at the time worshiped idols. Muhammad and a band of his devotees in A.D. 622 were obliged to flee Mecca in fear for their lives. Their flight to Medina, an oasis to the north (also located in modern-day Saudi Arabia), is remembered by Muslims as the Hegira. Muhammad's teachings were welcomed in Medina, and he was made a local governor. Later, he was able to return to Mecca.

Today, a journey or "pilgrimage" to Mecca is a key requirement of Islam. The Arabic term *Islam* implies submission to God's will.

Muslims, members of the Islamic faith, follow the teachings of the *Qur'an* (Koran). The Qur'an is a compilation of teachings presented by the prophet Muhammad as revelations to him from *Allah* (God) through an angel. These teachings were assembled and written down by followers during and after Muhammad's death in A.D. 632. They include not only spiritual text but also writings pertaining to legal, military, social, and business practices. Governments in Islamic countries base their laws on Islamic law, called the *sharia.*

There are differences among followers of Islam. Some tailor their daily lives strictly to Qur'anic tradition. This affects their food, dress, and other customs as well as their worship. Other Muslims are more liberal, following the basic requirements of worship and holy day observations but not adhering to every instruction of the Qur'an.

There are two separate branches of Islam. Most Muslims around the world are Sunnites. A minority worldwide—but the majority in Iran—are Shiites. The division between them dates to the early centuries of Islam and is rooted in the question of succession in leadership. Shiites believe the Prophet Muhammad chose his son-in-law Ali ibn Abu Talib to be the civil as well as spiritual leader of Islam after his death. This leader is known to Shiites as the *imam.* To Shiites, only descendants of Ali are qualified to serve as the imam.

Sunnites, on the other hand, honor the line of succession that began with Abu Bakr, a follower who was elected caliph after Muhammad died. Ali, Muhammad's son-in-law, decided not to contest the election, in the interest of maintaining a united Islam. Within a few generations, though, the two factions were at violent odds. A corrupt early caliph named Yezid sent a massive army against a small band led by Husain, one of Ali's sons, in the year 680. In the desert of Kerbala in what is today Iraq, the caliph's army killed Husain and virtually annihilated his force.

The slaughter of Husain provoked a fiercely proud tradition among the Shiites. They consider Sunnites to be followers of an uncouth, counterfeit line of caliphs, and themselves to be defenders of justice and of the true Muslim faith. In late-twentieth-century Iran, this ingrained division would play a key role in breeding revolution. Shah Pahlavi would come to be regarded as a successor of the despised Yezid. Ayatollah Khomeini would be perceived as an avenger of Husain and the true spiritual leader of Iran.

A succession of invaders and rulers changed the shape and character of the Persian Empire during the twelve centuries after the Arabs came to power. Different cities rose in prominence. Eventually, Persia roughly could be defined as what is today Iran. Tehran, initially only a village, became its capital.

Shiism became Persia's official religion in 1501 with the rise to power of the Safavid Dynasty. Shiism remains the dominant religion of Iranians, despite many changes in political and military domination throughout the past five centuries.

In 1794, a powerful chieftain named Aga Muhammad Qajar seized control. The Qajar Dynasty he established ruled Persia until 1925. It was led by a succession of *shahs*. Wielding total power, each shah was deemed king of kings and "the shadow of God on earth."[1]

Persian shahs during the nineteenth century found themselves at war with Russia and at odds with England over territorial claims. As a result, Persia had to make important land concessions. Outsiders—Russia, England, and Turkey—began to influence Persia's internal affairs.

During the 1700s and 1800s, the country's religious teachers, called *ulema*, acquired a special leadership role. They became, in a sense, watchdogs over the policies of the ruler. Eventually, they emerged not just as Islamic scholars but as political critics of the Qajar shahs. They spoke out against trends and events—particularly foreign influence in Persian affairs—that they believed were weakening Islam within their society. History was aligning the forces that, in the twentieth century, would wage a climactic struggle for control over Iran: Muslim fundamentalism versus a secular form of government.

The ulema acquired more than just popular respect for their intimate knowledge of the Qur'an. They acquired financial power. They received an income for their work as teachers. They also received a share of the taxes that Islam requires of its people, and they were in charge of distributing contributions to the needy. By the end of the nineteenth century, the ulema were a powerful group, both in influencing public thinking and in controlling a significant share of the country's economy. They exercised their power apart from—and often in disagreement with—the government.

Opposition to the Qajar Dynasty grew, led by Muslim clerics. The religious leaders sensed that their long-established control over certain matters was being challenged. They also were alarmed that the shahs were selling control over important Persian assets to foreigners. The rulers sold interests in Persian banks and railroads, for example, to European entrepreneurs. Business and social affairs seemed increasingly contrary to the ideals of Islam. But what could the ulema do against the shah and his formidable military?

In the early 1890s, these dissidents proved that a compelling statement could be made with their pocketbooks. Nasir al-Din Shah, the shah at the time, sold an English company a monopoly over tobacco sales in his country. The agreement granted the Imperial Tobacco Corporation all rights to tobacco production and sales in Persia. Roused to fury by Shiite leaders, the people staged demonstrations against the British monopoly in what became known as the Tobacco Rebellion. The leading Muslim cleric, Mirza Hasan Shirazi, brought the issue to a head by declaring that the use of tobacco by Muslims was illegal. Persians—traditionally heavy users of tobacco products—stopped smoking. The Persian tobacco market collapsed, the shah was forced to withdraw the agreement, and the British lost their monopoly.

This was no minor footnote in Iranian history books. It was, in a sense, a turning point. It showed that the ulema—not the government—commanded the genuine mood of the Persian people. In time, Khomeini and other Muslim religious leaders would exercise their control to bring about a new and very different form of government.

In 1906, the ulema were instrumental in forcing the shah to allow a representative body of government, or parliament, called the *Majlis*. The shah also consented to a constitution that embraced Islamic law. The new arrangement was short-lived. By the early 1910s, Persia's internal dilemma was overshadowed by ominous international developments. World War I broke out in Europe. Although the Middle East was not a major theatre of combat, it was important to the warring European nations because of its oil reserves. During the war years (1914–1918), British and Russian forces occupied Persia and battled the Turks, who were allied with Germany.

Between 1921 and 1926, a Cossack military leader, Reza Khan, rose to power in Persia with British support. Cossacks were famous cavalry fighters of lower Russia and the Caucasus. Khan had joined the army as a teenager and had earned an exceptional reputation for valiant military service. As a Cossack commander, he helped oust the Soviets who occupied much of his homeland. The reigning Qajar shah by this time had fled the country, and Khan took his place. He crowned himself (literally) shah of a new dynasty: Pahlavi.

As might be expected in such disorderly circumstances, Reza Shah Pahlavi, who had been mild-mannered as a child, grew to be a hard military man and a formidable ruler. He subdued tribal leaders who posed a threat to his authority. Peasants never forgot the time the fearsome shah, who stood six-foot-three, ordered one of their donkeys shot because it had wandered onto royal property. Shiite clergy never forgot the time he horse-whipped a *mullah*; the clergyman had criticized the shah's wife after she accidentally exposed her veiled face at the holy shrine of Fatima in the city of Qom.

The shah was poorly educated—a source of personal embarrassment that made him determined to educate his children well. Nonetheless, he had a progressive vision for his country and sought to Westernize it. In 1935, he proclaimed that Persia was to be known as *Iran*. The word commemorates the Aryans, a nomadic people who roamed the region as early as four thousand years ago. (The word *Persia*, by contrast, had derived from a Greek place name, Parsa.) Pahlavi changed the name because he wanted his land to be recognized not for its humiliating period of control by outsiders, but for its independence and for its potential to be an important nation of the twentieth century.

Pahlavi knew the ulema would oppose his policies of modernization. To accomplish what he wanted would require cooperation with industrial nations—the West. It also would require adapting certain Western-style institutions, such as secular (nonreligious) courts, and making changes in education. This would erode much of the power the ulema had established for themselves as judges and teachers. They were sure to resist.

By the beginning of World War II in 1939, the shah had achieved national improvements, notably in the Iranian transportation system. The new Trans-Iranian Railway was something of a monument to his progressive ideas. He also was nurturing industrial development and improvements in education, including six years of required instruction for girls as well as boys, and new schools and colleges. A seemingly minor change—but one that symbolized the coming struggle between the government and Islam—was his abolition of the requirement that women veil their faces in public, as was customary among Muslims. This type of modernization alarmed devout Shiites, who complained that the law of Islam was being cast aside. They accused the shah of ruining their religious heritage. Most of their protests were peaceful, but when the shah sensed that some of the ulema and their supporters were becoming aggressive, he responded forcefully. Demonstrators were beaten and jailed. Some were even killed by soldiers who were sent to disperse the protests.

But Reza Shah Pahlavi discovered that the Iranian people's loyalty to their Muslim leaders was greater than their interest in his vision for the future. It was one thing to discontinue the Muslim requirement for women to wear veils in public. It was quite another to take charge of trust and gift funds accumulated by the ulema. The people undermined his policies by continuing to support the Shiite clergy financially. Muslim journalist Mohamed Heikal surmised in his book *Iran: The Untold Story*, "A Persian citizen may be prepared to cheat the tax-collector, but not his ayatollah." [2]

As the Second World War unfolded, the shah claimed neutrality but seemed to show signs of supporting the German/Italian/Japanese Axis. Regardless of whether he actually favored the Axis powers, the Axis's opponents (the Soviet Union and Great Britain, known as the Allies) suspected he did. Their forces once more occupied Iran. Reza Shah Pahlavi was forced to abandon his throne. His oldest son Muhammad Reza took his place in 1941. Reza Shah Pahlavi died in exile in South Africa three years later.

The new leader, who had been schooled in Switzerland, was only twenty-one years old at the time. His youth hardly mattered, for he had little to do during the years of occupation. After the war ended in 1945, he and his country became caught up in superpower politics. Eastern European countries controlled by the Soviet Union squared off against the United States and Western Europe in what became known as the Cold War. Iran, like many other non-European nations, was courted by both sides.

Iran under the Pahlavis made progress in modernization, but the royal court indulged in glaring excesses—lavish living and the granting of political favors. This was especially true under the younger shah. While many of his people lived in poverty, he was viewed as a flamboyant head of state, a playboy. During the early years of his reign, Pahlavi became an object of derision to an obscure Shiite cleric in an obscure Iranian town. The two men were destined to clash one day for control of their country.

From its beginning, Iran, like many other Islamic nations, has been marked deeply by two contrasting characteristics: religious fervor and royal indulgence. Islam demands stern morality and principles. Yet, from the seventh century into the late 1900s, the royalty of many Middle Eastern countries ruled with an extravagance that, in some circumstances, was shocking. Kings and court favorites reveled while commoners and clerics seethed—a sure formula for upheaval.

3

The Scholar
From Khomein

Ayatollah Ruhollah Khomeini likely will be remembered as one of the most puzzling national leaders in history. Facts of his childhood are sketchy. When he became a teacher, his followers studied his lectures and writings and held him in awe, but he remained a private, aloof individual. To the Western world, he was hardly known at all until the final dramatic decade of his long life. During those fleeting years in power, he held private audiences with many Iranians but rarely was seen in public. Foreign journalists frequently questioned whether he was in failing health. What, exactly, was his role in Iranian affairs after the revolution? What were his plans?

Even his birthday is uncertain. It has been stated alternately as May 17 or September 24, 1902. Certain records indicate the birth year was 1900 or 1901. At the time, Iran still was called Persia. In any case, he was born in Khomein, a remote village at the edge of the Iranian Desert some two hundred miles south of Tehran. The name *Khomein* means "two jars" in Arabic. His given name was Ruhollah Musawi. *Ruhollah* means "soul of God."

The family lived in a house of mud brick. They were not wealthy, but they were considered special in the village because they claimed as one of their ancestors none other than the prophet Muhammad. You will undoubtedly notice in pictures of Ayatollah Khomeini that the turban atop his head was black, not white. Men who are descended from Muhammad are entitled to wear this black turban.

Ruhollah's grandfather Sayid Ahmed was a native of Kashmir in India who went to Persia for his education in the mid-1800s. Sayid Ahmed settled down in Khomein. He came to be considered a *mullah* in the village, a title of respect that signified a community leader. Sayid's son Sayid Mustafa also grew to become a mullah.

Ruhollah was the second son born to Sayid Mustafa and his wife, Sadiqeh. Sadiqeh, as was customary in Persian society, was probably only in her early teens at the time of their marriage. Several children were born to the couple before Ruhollah; all but one died in childhood.

When Ruhollah was an infant, his father was killed. Details of his death are unclear. Some believed he was slain by robbers while on a journey to Iraq. Others said he was stabbed by agents of the family's landlord when Mustafa argued with them about the rent. Speculation also suggested assassination by religious or political opponents—possibly by agents of the country's reigning dynasty, the Qajar regime. Another account held that in his role as mullah of the town, Mustafa had ordered a man executed for disobeying a Muslim custom, and a friend of the condemned man killed Mustafa in revenge.

Ruhollah's mother could no longer support him. She sent him to live with his aunt. At age four, he began to study the Qur'an. It was in this way that he learned to read and write, while also learning the teachings of Muhammad. His was a rigid Shiite upbringing. His family had little respect for Muslims who did not follow the Shiite lineage, and they held animosity toward non-Muslims. They believed their government's relations with Great Britain and other Western powers were undermining Islam.

Ruhollah was said to be a bright, eager student. This meant, among other things, that he grew to be a bright, eager defender of Islamic traditions. He also grew to be sturdy and independent—"a self-sufficient, tough little boy," according to one chronicler.[3]

When he was about fifteen, Ruhollah was orphaned. Both his mother and aunt died within a few months of each other. He went to live with his older brother, Basandidah Musawi, himself a devout Shiite and mullah. Basandidah continued Ruhollah's Qur'anic instruction and was pleased to observe that his brother's sharp mind was focused on strict Muslim teachings. "I was older than Ruhollah, but he was always wiser," Basandidah later would say.[4]

At nineteen, Ruhollah was off to Arak, a city of modest size situated in a fruit-growing region about 140 miles southwest of Tehran. There, he intensified his religious studies at a Muslim school, called a *madreseh*. His mentor was a noted Islamic scholar, Ayatollah Abdul Karim Haeri. Haeri himself had been trained by Shirazi, the famous cleric who had declared tobacco illegal a generation earlier. Ruhollah was being groomed to follow in Haeri's footsteps as one of the region's principal Islamic theologians.

In 1922, Ayatollah Haeri moved to the city of Qom, an ancient center of the Shiite faith located in a dry, dusty region about 100 miles south of the capital. Haeri was invited there to take over the local school and develop it into a respected Muslim training center. The school became known as the Madraseh Faizieh. Ruhollah, who accompanied him to Qom, would become one of Haeri's most impressive students. He showed remarkable skill in debate and analysis. In time, he became one of the center's prominent teachers. He would be widely known as a Muslim scholar.

Qom is a city of special importance to Shiite Muslims because the historic tomb of Fatimah Ma'suma is there. Fatimah was the sister of Ali al-Rida, an ancient imam—a holy man descended from the prophet Muhammad's son-in-law Ali ibn Abu Talib. For centuries, Shiites had made pilgrimages to Qom to pay their respects at Fatimah's tomb.

It was at Qom that Ruhollah married. When he was twenty-five, he asked an older friend for the matrimonial hand of the friend's fourteen-year-old daughter, Khadijah. According to author Mohamed Heikal, "When she heard of the marriage proposal she protested. She had no wish to marry a mullah, her ambition being to marry a government official and go to live in Tehran." [5] But she consented after being convinced in a dream to accept Ruhollah as her husband.

Shortly after the revolution, Heikal wrote of Khadijah:

> Khomeini's wife is a woman of great strength of character, energy and charm. When he was deported from Qom in 1963 and dumped on the Turkish frontier, Khomeini told her not to try to follow him, but she ignored his instructions and made her way to Najaf [in Iraq, where he ultimately found exile]. [6]

Over the years, they would have eight children. Five survived infancy. As we will see later, his oldest surviving son, Mustafa, died mysteriously in 1977—an event that contributed to a growing frenzy for revolution in Iran. His son Ahmed would play a role in the takeover of the U.S. Embassy in Tehran in October 1979 and would serve as his father's primary aide after the revolution. One of his daughters, Zahra Mustafavi, would become the leader of the Women's Organization of the Islamic Republic.

It should not be assumed the young scholar at Qom immersed himself in Islamic theology and nothing else. The writings of Aristotle and Plato, the famous ancient Greek philosophers, influenced him. He became a teacher of philosophy. He also became a poet and began to write books—twenty-one, eventually. Meanwhile, he was deeply interested not only in the practical and legal aspects of the Qur'an but in the mystical aspects of the religion. Mysticism combined the study of Qur'anic law with "an emotional experience achieved by spiritual contact with God's cosmic presence," explained Daniel Brumberg, author of *Reinventing Khomeini*. Self-denial is part of this experience. "By denying all but the most basic needs—sometimes to the point of physical suffering—and by engaging in simple but passionate forms of prayer that can produce trancelike effects, the mystic, or Sufi . . . loses his 'self' in the 'Essence' of God, the most pure form of which is light itself."[7]

His teachers and colleagues were very impressed by Ruhollah at Qom. "Over the years," wrote historian Dilip Hiro, "he established himself as a learned teacher of ethics and philosophy as well as an extraordinarily disciplined and orderly person. He was particularly noted for interrelating ethical and spiritual problems with contemporary social issues, and urging his students to regard it as part of their religious duty to work for the solution of current social problems."[8]

Ruhollah was twenty-eight when he journeyed to Mecca, Islam's holy city in what is today Saudi Arabia. All Muslims are required to make at least one pilgrimage to Mecca in their lifetimes. It was about this time that he took for himself a surname,

Khomeini, connoting the town of his birth. This was in accordance with Shiite custom, which called for religious teachers to be known by their birthplace.

Under Haeri's leadership, the school at Qom acquired a notable reputation as a center of Islamic training. As the school flourished, so did the city, nurtured in large part by Haeri's personal prosperity. He was instrumental in starting a hospital. In time, Qom became a hub of Shiite theology.

SHIITE CLERGY

There are no clear equivalents of "priests," "rabbis," or "bishops" among Shiite clergy. As we learned in an earlier chapter, there are teachers and interpreters of Islamic law, called *ulema*. Until modern times, the ulema were, for practical purposes, Persia's educators. Over the centuries, the ulema evolved into a special class. The people looked to them as their local authorities. The ulema collected and distributed offerings—which gave them considerable power—and they commanded a distinctive form of respect. Because of their knowledge of Islamic law, members of the ulema typically are selected as Iran's judges.

Mullahs are clergymen who serve Shiite communities as teachers and preachers. Lower-ranking mullahs are not qualified to interpret Islamic laws. *Mujtahids* are more advanced Islamic scholars. Some acquire a superior status called *hojatalislam*. A select few of these highest-ranking mujtahids eventually are recognized as *ayatollahs*.

Clerics specially trained as interpreters of Islamic law are the *fuqaha* (the singular form is *faqih*). Islamic law is called the *sharia*. A *faqih* is authorized to make binding decisions in questions concerning Islamic law.

The word *imam* has two meanings. Some Muslims loosely refer to local clergymen and prayer leaders as imams. However, to most Shiites in Iran, the term has far greater significance. Imams are Muhammad's legitimate successors and thus are the most sacred interpreters of the Qur'an. According to Shiite tradition, twelve imams were born during the first few centuries after the death of Ali. The twelfth, regarded as the "hidden" imam, is believed to have vanished more than a thousand years ago but someday will reappear on Earth. His reappearance supposedly will bring justice throughout the world.

Those who follow this belief in the twelve imams are known as the Twelver sect of Shiism. Twelver Shiism is Iran's official religion.

Haeri died in 1937. Replacing such an important scholar was a difficult challenge. Not until 1944 was his successor installed, another highly regarded teacher named Ayatollah Muhammad Husayn Borujerdi. The school and city grew to even greater prominence during Borujerdi's fifteen years of leadership.

Khomeini himself played no small role in the success of the Madreseh Faizieh at Qom. He taught at the school for three decades, until the early 1960s. An excellent instructor, he developed a large following of students who remembered and respected him long after they heard his lectures. Charisma seemed an odd trait for an individual of such a cold nature. As one historian described, "He was a forbidding man who never offered more than a smile in public to express his pleasure in anybody or anything." Yet, Khomeini was considered "one of the most intelligent teachers in Qom." [9]

He had come to believe that strict adherence to Qur'anic teachings was of utmost importance in life. This, he insisted to his students, required concentrated self-control. Khomeini believed everything was either good or evil. He disdained all forms of what he considered distractions from pure thinking. Distractions, to him, included not only such indulgences as alcoholic drink—forbidden in Islamic countries—but even music. Music, he claimed, merely serves to numb one's thoughts. Therefore, it must be grouped among the evil things of life.

Although many non-Shiites, especially Westerners, scoff at such strictness, his students respected him because he appeared to practice what he preached. Khomeini as a young man adopted a simple lifestyle and followed it into his old age. For example, he preferred to sleep on a blanket, called a *doshak*, on the floor. This personal custom dated to his years as a student at Qom, when he was obliged to find sleeping space in the mosque because he could not afford lodging elsewhere.

Khomeini frequently voiced the Muslim principle that people who were well-to-do should assist the poor. He held that governments should take care of their underprivileged citizens—and he believed the Pahlavi government of Iran was doing far too little.

Social justice was a principle he would preach throughout his life. Furthermore, he pointed to corruption in the government as a sign that the Pahlavi regime was evil, not good.

The contempt he held for the Pahlavis, father and son, would lead Ayatollah Khomeini eventually to depart from the stance taken by other Shiite clerics. They, too, believed in strict Qur'anic ideals. However, they did not believe that they should take an active role in political matters. Khomeini disagreed. Islam, he contended, was political as well as religious. "In fact," he wrote, "if one refers to the practice of [Muhammad], which are the main Muslim texts, one sees that they deal as much with politics, government, the struggle against tyrants, as with prayers." [10] Later, after being released from one of several periods of confinement for his radical activities, he would state his opinion emphatically: "All of Islam is politics." [11]

Interestingly, Ayatollah Borujerdi strongly discouraged teachers and students in Qom from involving themselves in politics. He went so far as to dismiss politically active ulema. Khomeini, despite his strong feelings about the Pahlavi regime's policies, did not challenge his leader as long as Borujerdi was alive. He expressed his views to his students, but he did not criticize Pahlavi publicly during the years when Borujerdi was his superior.

With ever-increasing scrutiny, however, he noted recurring indications that Pahlavi posed a menace to Islamic authority. He criticized Pahlavi's literacy program that sent educated military personnel into rural villages to teach youngsters, for Khomeini believed all teaching should be done by Muslim clerics. He felt that by granting women certain freedoms, the government was corrupting them. And he openly suspected that Pahlavi's land reforms, which affected the mullahs' financial security, were drawn up by the Israelis.

Khomeini would be in his sixties before the time was right for him to openly press his case against Shah Pahlavi. When that time came, the shah would find him to be a bold, baffling, and unbending opponent.

4

Shah Pahlavi's Quest for Glory

Muhammad Reza Shah Pahlavi, it might be argued, was not exactly the callous, extravagant leader depicted by the revolutionaries who hated him. Handsome and skilled in social graces, he was indeed something of a playboy. He married three times—the last time, in 1959, to a wealthy, French-educated Iranian beauty barely half his age. From the start of his reign, though, he seemed to recognize the plight of his people. Only twenty-one when he succeeded his father in 1941, he refused to assume the crown, stating that he had no desire to be king of "a nation of beggars." His detractors among Iran's Muslim clergy sarcastically discounted this as a ploy to cast himself as a virtuous, humble leader while in reality he was, in their eyes, a misguided, oppressive dictator. In either case, Pahlavi was an intelligent young man with an excellent education. He understood that major reforms were in order if Iran was to avert internal disaster. He did not permit his coronation to take place until 1967, long after he launched his reform efforts—and only a dozen years before the revolution would depose him.

What Pahlavi wanted for Iran was what his father had wanted: a modern, industrial empire that would be as glorious, in its own time period, as ancient Persia had been. To create it, he needed help from Western industrial nations, and he needed money. Iran had a means by which to obtain both: oil. This valuable resource had been discovered in 1908 by an early petroleum entrepreneur from Australia, William Knox D'Arcy, in the Khuzistan region of the country. With help from Great Britain, D'Arcy established an enterprise that became known as the Anglo-Iranian Oil Company (AIOC). Over the years, Great Britain obtained a majority interest in the company. In other words, most of the profit from the sale of Iran's oil went to British investors. This was one example of the foreign involvement that aroused the resentment of Muslim clergymen.

Great Britain and its allies relied heavily on Iranian oil for their ships, planes, tanks, and trucks during World War II. After the war, the worldwide demand for petroleum was high and the country's oil fields thrived. Iran exported more than 30 million tons of oil in 1950, making it one of the leading oil-producing countries in the world. While the middle and upper classes of Iranians benefited from this oil boom, thousands of poor citizens still languished in poverty.

By this time, the United States also had taken an interest in Iranian oil reserves. The Cold War had gripped the globe, with the United States and the Soviet Union vying for influence in diverse regions. Fearing the Soviets would win control of Iran and its oil, the U.S. government quietly became involved in Iranian politics and military affairs. It supported Muslim groups that disliked the Soviets, sent advisors to help Pahlavi's armed forces, and sold him weapons.

Neither Pahlavi nor the Iranian parliament, the Majlis, was happy watching most of the country's oil profits being siphoned off by foreign interests. There seemed little they could do to change the situation, though. Not so resigned were an aging nationalist activist named Muhammad Mosaddiq and an Islamic leader named Ayatollah Seyed Abol Qassem Kashani. They marshaled opposition to the AIOC, demanding that the country's oil industry be taken away from foreign interests, or *nationalized*. To them and thousands of their followers, the foreigner entrepreneurs were causing two major problems for Iran: They were hampering the country's economy and they were undermining Islamic traditions. Ruhollah Khomeini, at the time a teacher at Qom, was among those who held this view.

The public demand for oil nationalization turned violent. Terrorists assassinated Prime Minister Ali Razmara and other government officials. Alarmed, the Majlis moved to grant their demand, passing a nationalization law. Great Britain tried unsuccessfully to block the action through international legal channels. The AIOC was forced to shut down its operations.

Mosaddiq became prime minister of Iran in May 1951. Both inside and outside Iran, he was perceived as a contender for Pahlavi's authority. If successful, he gradually could assume the government's policy-making role, leaving Pahlavi as nothing more than a royal figurehead. Mosaddiq made dramatic progress toward that end. For example, he managed to bring the country's military under the control of the Majlis; previously, it had been under Pahlavi's direct command. Mosaddiq also began work on land reforms that would redistribute wealth among the classes.

In response to Iran's nationalization of oil, the AIOC led an international boycott of Iranian oil purchases. This badly damaged Iran's economy. The situation was made worse by the fact that Iranians were not well trained to operate their own oil industry. For years, refinery technology and management had been performed by foreign petroleum professionals.

Among Iranians, anti-American sentiment now was on the rise, along with anti-Pahlavi sentiment. Demonstrations were staged in 1953, and the army had to be sent in to quell the unrest. At the same time, opposition was being organized against the prime minister. A group of army officers, unhappy with Mosaddiq's military changes, began to plot his overthrow. The United States, fearing the rise of Iran's Communist party, Tudeh, lent the conspirators the support of the Central Intelligence Agency (CIA). Pahlavi endorsed the plot. The first coup attempt in August 1953 failed, prompting Pahlavi to flee briefly to Italy. Within days, though, Mosaddiq was toppled, and Pahlavi recovered his authority.

In the aftermath of this turmoil, the United States established a key partnership role with Iran. It acquired more than 40 percent of the control of the old Anglo-Iranian Oil Company. Along with Israel, it helped Pahlavi organize a strong security force, SAVAK, to tighten his control.

Possibly more than anything else, this sequence of events in the early 1950s set the stage for the coming revolution. Certainly, it defined the United States as "the enemy" in the minds of Muslim fundamentalists in Iran. Wrote Middle East commentator Lawrence Ziring: "What had begun as a commercial affair involving a foreign-owned oil company quickly escalated into a political and ideological confrontation of enormous complexity, with great consequences for Iran, the Middle East, and the rest of the world."[12]

While developments such as these riled the Muslim leadership in Iran, they were part of Pahlavi's plan for modernizing his nation. Iran had valuable oil reserves. The United States had technology, military equipment, and valuable industrial advisors. By using Iran's natural resources and strategic foreign alliances, Pahlavi believed he could create a modern-day empire that would be more impressive, in many ways, than ancient Persia.

But he recognized that Iran's Islamic clergy were a powerful class to be reckoned with. He must maintain peace with them, if at all possible. He was, after all, a Muslim himself, if not a particularly zealous one. To forge a bond—or at least the appearance of a bond—with the Muslim leadership, he visited Islamic shrines and made the solemn pilgrimage to Mecca. He brought aspects of Western culture to the country, but he made some concessions to devout Muslim leaders who complained, for example, of the loose morals depicted in movies being shown in Iranian cinemas.

Pahlavi's reform strategy took a momentous turn in 1962 when he declared a "White Revolution." This was a sweeping social and economic reform program. It included, among other features, land reform, permission for non-Muslims to vie for elective office, profit-sharing for the working class, an expansion of education and health care into rural areas, and voting privileges for women. To Western societies, these were seen as positive signs of a progressive government. Iran's Shiite leaders, however, were irate—not just over the liberalized election policies, which they thought would corrupt the character of Muslim women, but over the land issues. Muslim clerics relied for their financial security and power not on the peasants they vocally defended, but on donations from more moneyed, middle-class families. In effect, Pahlavi's "White Revolution" threatened to upset these contributions. Meanwhile, the shah's rural literacy initiative tended to undermine the community authority of the religious educators.

It was at this juncture that Ruhollah Khomeini began to emerge as a militant Muslim leader. He fiercely condemned his government's weakening of Islamic influence in society and its ties with the United States. Looking back, some historians consider this a surprising development. Dilip Hiro, in his book *Iran Under the Ayatollahs*, observed that Khomeini "was by training, and inclination, a theological teacher, not a politician. He was certainly not a revolutionary, nor even a serious student of revolution."[13] That would change in the coming years.

While Khomeini and other Iranian clerics were concerned primarily with the heritage and lineage of the prophet Muhammad, Shah Pahlavi was more interested in the heritage and lineage of the bygone Persian Empire. It has been suggested that Pahlavi considered himself, in a sense, the modern heir to King Cyrus— a role that obligated him to revive and even surpass the glory of ancient Persia. As he concentrated on Iran's development and future, Pahlavi was ever mindful of Persia's glorious past.

By the early 1970s, the shah justifiably was boasting that Iran had become a unique combination of ancient grandeur and modern progress. In October 1971, Iran was host to an extraordinary twenty-five-hundredth anniversary of the Persian Empire's establishment by Cyrus the Great. Foreign heads of state and dignitaries gathered to celebrate at Persepolis, site of ancient ruins dating to the era of Darius. Pahlavi welcomed two dozen visiting kings, princes, and presidents, plus scores of less eminent guests. They were housed in richly furnished, air-conditioned tents and feasted on sumptuous delights prepared by internationally noted chefs. So prestigious was the affair among world leaders that a royal flap developed over who would be seated in the most honored positions at banquets. (When Pahlavi awarded the highest designation to Ethiopian Emperor Haile Selassie, French President Georges Pompidou snubbed the celebration, sending his nation's prime minister in his place.)

It was a lavish exercise in pomp and spectacle that cost several hundred-million dollars. Shah Pahlavi made a curious, self-flattering speech at Cyrus's archaic tomb. He proclaimed to his historic idol: "We are here at the moment when Iran renews its pledge to History to bear witness to the immense gratitude of

an entire people to you, immortal Hero of History, founder of
the world's oldest empire, great liberator of all time, worthy son
of mankind. . . . Sleep on in peace forever, for we are awake and
we remain to watch over your glorious heritage." [14]

Many Iranians failed to take pride in their country, however.
They were appalled by the Hollywood-style production at
Persepolis. Ayatollah Khomeini by this time was waging a
long-distance war of propaganda against the shah from exile in
Iraq. He lambasted the anniversary event as grotesquely extravagant, in view of the plight of Iran's poor classes. He and other
critics also observed that the grand celebration at Persepolis was
a secular gala, which proved that the shah was little concerned
about the role of Islam in Iran. "Sovereignty belongs to God
alone," Khomeini insisted. "Resurgence against the Pahlavi
dynasty is demanded of the people by the sacred laws." [15] He
further proclaimed, "Anyone who organizes or participates in
these festivals is a traitor to Islam and the Iranian nation." [16]

Sentiment against the shah and against Western influence
in Iran was growing, especially among students, agitated by
Muslim leaders. Gradually, these feelings would spread from
students and intellectuals to the discontented poor and working
classes—even those who were comparatively well to do. It
was no secret that the royal family and the upper class were
acquiring great wealth from their financial interests in industri-
alization, while an estimated 40 percent of Iranians during the
1970s lived in poverty, despite the oil boom. It was no secret that
foreigners brought to Iran to supply much of the skilled labor
force received higher pay than Iranian workers. And it was no
secret that the shah's support of Israel ran counter to the attitude
of most Islamic nations, and of most Iranians.

Resentment was building across a broad segment of the population. In the mosques, the ulema laced sermons with political
criticism and denunciations of the materialism that had become
rampant under the shah's rule. Their messages appealed especially
to the poor and to political and religious radicals.

Shah Pahlavi did not seem to realize it, but he was losing his grip on the nation he ruled. To some extent, he in fact played the tyrant's role of which Khomeini accused him. For example, the shah decided certain matters that should have been legislated by the Majlis. His government kept a heavy hand on political opposition, on the media, on commerce, and on education. Those in positions of power under the shah likewise ignored the sentiments of others and handled matters as they pleased, sometimes infuriating the population.

More and more Iranians wanted major changes to take place. But how could they make that happen? Changes could not come through appeals to the royal court. Therefore, the people turned their gaze to Iraq, where a defiant member of Iran's religious leadership was living in exile, advocating a new Iran that would have no shah at its head.

5

Setting the Stage
for Revolution

A s we've seen, even before the Pahlavi era, some members of
the ulema looked with skepticism and eventually with open
contempt toward the regime in Tehran. Islamic law, they felt,
should be central to government. The Pahlavi government,
however, seemed to be sidestepping the ancient traditions and
relegating Islamic authority to a secondary or separate role in
Iranian society.

Ruhollah Khomeini agreed with the ulema. By the end of
World War II, he had become recognized as a teacher of the
hojatalislam rank. "This meant that he could now collect his
own circle of disciples, who would accept his interpretation of
the Sharia and hadith (the sayings and actions of Prophet
Muhammad)," wrote Dilip Hiro. "A way was now prepared for
his elevation to the next level: an ayatollah." [17]

Students marveled at his knowledge and his austere lifestyle,
and wondered at his unfathomable character. He lectured, by
one account, "without looking at his audience, and his aloofness
while teaching was part and parcel of the aloofness that was
variously regarded with admiration, fear, or dislike by other
teachers at Qom." [18] Outside class, he was essentially a very
private individual, usually unsociable and at times unapproachable. He often sought solitude. This aspect of his personality
contributed a magnetic mystique to his emerging popularity.

Khomeini was becoming evermore opposed to the Pahlavi
regime. He had criticized the early reform measures of
Reza Shah Pahlavi in the 1930s, claiming they were part of a
Westernizing process that undermined the people's Islamic
identity. He considered the younger Pahlavi an even greater
threat to Islam because of the close ties the shah forged with
Great Britain and the United States. By 1953, Khomeini's
contempt for the government was deeply set, although he abided
by the wishes of his school's director, Ayatollah Borujerdi,
that the Muslim leaders and students in Qom refrain from
political activism. When Pahlavi made a trip that year to Qom,
Khomeini refused to pay him formal respect. Across the
Middle East, Israeli-Arab tensions were at a dangerous stage

over the explosive Palestinian issue. Khomeini accused Pahlavi of forming an unspoken alliance with the United States and Israel, Muslims' avowed enemy.

He became a prolific author during his years at Qom. In the early 1940s, he penned *The Unveiling of the Secrets* (*Kashf al-Asrar*), in which he bluntly condemned the behavior and policies of the recently deposed shah. Khomeini considered the elder shah an intolerable dictator who was antagonizing the Muslim leadership.

WHO WERE KHOMEINI'S FOLLOWERS?

Intellectuals were among the earliest protesters against the Pahlavi regime in the 1950s and 1960s. They expressed their opposition effectively in pamphlets, letters, and other writings. They would join Ayatollah Khomeini in pressing for the shah's overthrow.

Meanwhile, the *mustazafin*, Iran's poor, naturally were attracted to Khomeini's demands for an equitable distribution of wealth. Even when oil sales pumped up the country's economy, little of the income found its way down to the lower classes of society. Basically, those close to the oil industry and the Pahlavi regime simply grew richer, and the division between rich and poor deepened and broadened into a dangerous chasm.

Those parts of Khomeini's support base—the intellectuals and the downtrodden—were predictable. One of the unusual aspects of Khomeini's rise to power, on the other hand, was his appeal to middle-class university students, including young women. In Western countries, students were rebelling *against* moral authority. But in Iran, they seemed to clamor for the more strict brand of Shiite authority urged by the exiled ayatollah.

Khomeini also attracted the attention of militant Muslim leaders elsewhere. Notably, Yasir Arafat of the Palestine Liberation Organization (PLO) paid him a personal visit.

Clearly, opposition to the regime of the shah was becoming general in nature. It eventually spanned most sectors of Iranian society. But while Iran's religious leadership preached the fire of revolution, it was the youth who would carry it out. Most of the militants who would overrun the U.S. Embassy in Tehran in 1979 would be university students.

Later works included several law books. These were not openly political in tone, but Khomeini took the opportunity to encourage readers to aid the downtrodden of society and to oppose government corruption. In retrospect, it seems clear that he was suggesting his growing distaste for the shah's son, Iran's new ruler. Khomeini likewise began expressing his belief that the ulema should have an overriding role in formulating government policies, since they knew more about Islamic law than politicians and administrators did.

Ayatollah Borujerdi, Khomeini's superior at the school in Qom, died in 1961. This marked a turning point in the younger cleric's life. Obedient to his master—for the most part, at any rate—he had shied away from political activity during his years at the Madraseh Faizieh. His books and his name, outside Qom, were not widely known. He was not of adequate stature among Iran's clergy to be considered as Borujerdi's successor. He soon attained the rank of ayatollah, however, after publication of his book *Tauzih al Masail*, or *Clarification of Points of the Sharia*. The word *ayatollah* means "reflection of Allah" or "miraculous sign of God." Khomeini's followers were devoted and growing in number. More than a thousand Muslim leaders over the years received instruction under him.

And now he felt the time had come to wage an assertive campaign against his country's government. Very soon, his name would be all too well known to Shah Pahlavi.

Pahlavi's "White Revolution"—also called the "Shah-People Revolution"—of 1962 brought the mounting dissent to a crisis. Khomeini issued a stinging criticism of the new liberal policies. He decried Pahlavi's affront to conventional religious leadership and his apparent leanings toward the United States and Israel. He broadened his attack into a general condemnation of Pahlavi's government, claiming that it failed to improve the lot of those who lived in poverty.

Pahlavi, in turn, challenged his detractors. In a January 1963 speech at Qom, he railed against "reactionary" Muslim leaders who opposed his vision for progress.

Escalation could hardly have been avoided. In March 1963, Twelver Shiites celebrated the anniversary of one of their martyrs, Ja'far al-Sadiq, the Sixth Imam, who is said to have been poisoned by Muslim enemies in 765. Khomeini took the occasion to issue another denunciation of the shah's regime. In response, government security agents invaded the Madraseh Faizieh. They destroyed property, took Khomeini and some of the other teachers into custody, and beat students, killing one of them. The clergy were soon released because of political pressure, but the affair drew wider attention to the movement of the religious protesters—particularly to Khomeini. Qom was becoming a seedbed of revolution, and Khomeini its planter. Copies of his speeches began to be widely read and quoted.

The "White Revolution" was changing the life and career of Ayatollah Khomeini. It was lifting him from his position of respect but relative obscurity to one of national notoriety. Until then, wrote one historian, no one could have imagined the stony-countenanced cleric from Khomein ever would amount to "anything but a high-ranking ayatollah." [19]

With Khomeini emerging as a spearhead, the ulema organized more demonstrations in June 1963. These coincided with the commemoration of Husain's historic martyrdom in 680. Some of them called for a *jihad*, or holy war, against the Pahlavi government.

At the Madraseh Faizieh, a major speech by the renegade Khomeini was anticipated by students and government officials alike. He did not disappoint them. Driven from his home to the Madreseh Faizieh in a Volkswagen, with students walking in procession in front and behind, he arrived to find a large audience gathering in the courtyards. When he began his speech, government agents cut off the power—not just to his microphone, but to the whole city. His supporters connected the sound system to an electrical generator. The ayatollah's address was broadcast outside the school premises over loudspeakers.

Khomeini spoke passionately of Husain's death. He compared the circumstances of 680 and those of 1963. Husain had done nothing to deserve persecution and death at the hands of the ruler, he said. "It seems to me that Yazid [Husain's mortal enemy] had a far more basic aim: He was opposed to the very existence of the family of the Prophet." Likewise, Khomeini argued, the student killed on the school grounds three months earlier had not deserved to die. "What had he done against the shah, against the government, against the tyrannical regime? We come to the conclusion that this regime also has a more basic aim: They are fundamentally opposed to Islam itself and the existence of the religious class."[20] He warned Pahlavi not to duplicate his father's fallacy in making agreements with Israel and other non-Muslim governments.

The Iranian military again were sent to arrest Khomeini. They took him to an army base in Tehran. By now, his name was widely recognized among Iranians who were dissatisfied with the Pahlavi government. They staged demonstrations—at times violent—in the capital, in Qom, and in several other cities. Soldiers confronted the protestors. Hundreds of people were killed and injured in the ensuing clashes. Pahlavi declared martial law until tensions eased.

This time, Khomeini and two other radical clergymen were kept in custody even after order had been restored. Alarmed by rumors that he was to be tried and executed, Iran's Muslim leaders—including some who disapproved of Khomeini's antagonistic strategy—implored Pahlavi not to punish him. Khomeini was never placed on trial, but he was detained until the following April.

For the next year, Khomeini made more critical speeches and worked to unite young dissidents. Meanwhile, he appealed to the poor across society, preaching that the Pahlavi government was doing little to help them. He also attracted members of the working class who feared foreign workers in Iranian industry might take their jobs. His messages were distributed on cassette tapes and leaflets. "He was no longer the somewhat unapproachable expert in philosophy and jurisprudence known only to the more academic mullahs," wrote historian Roy

Mottahedeh. "He was now a national figure, known to peasants as well as to talabehs as a man who had dared to publicly oppose the shah."[21]

All across Iran, there was broad and rising discontent, to be sure. It was aggravated in October 1964 when the government granted legal immunity to American military personnel stationed in Iran, as well as to their families. This was a diplomatic gesture apparently made by the shah in order to obtain a $200 million loan from the United States. Many Iranians were angered; even Pahlavi's supporters frowned on the new law. Khomeini's temper exploded. He proclaimed:

> They have reduced the Iranian people to a level lower than that of an American dog. If someone runs over a dog belonging to an American, he will be prosecuted. Even if the Shah himself were to run over a dog belonging to an American, he would be prosecuted. But if an American cook runs over the Shah, the head of state, no one will have the right to interfere with him.[22]

In effect, he stated, the country's parliament had committed an act of treason in passing this law. His accusations struck a cord with the people of Iran. Leaflets and tape recordings of his speech were widely distributed.

By now, Khomeini's deepening hatred for the United States appeared irreversible. He felt the same way toward the Pahlavi government, which he considered a puppet of Americans. His open criticism, which was attracting a disturbingly large following, could not be ignored. After Khomeini rejected the shah's appeals to moderate his criticism and demonstrated that he could not be silenced by force, he was exiled to Turkey in late 1964.

He soon proved too hot for the neighboring country to hold. Iranian students in Turkey organized public demonstrations in support of the ayatollah, who was becoming a martyr figure to young Iranians. Turkish leaders reacted by deporting him.

In October 1965, Khomeini relocated to Najaf, a Shiite

intellectual center in neighboring Iraq. It was a logical place for the ayatollah, located near the shrine of the prophet Muhammad's son-in-law, the imam Ali—the man Shiites believe was the rightful successor to the prophet. Although Najaf is not as important to Muslims as the holy city of Mecca in Saudi Arabia, many Shiite Muslims make solemn pilgrimages to Najaf.

Khomeini took up residence with his wife and oldest son in a modest home. "Like the Prophet and Ali," wrote historian Sandra Mackey, "he ate a meager diet of yogurt, cheese, lentils, and fruit. He slept on an ordinary rug spread on the floor. Day in and day out for almost thirteen years, he walked for twenty minutes; ate lunch and dinner; taught a small corps of students; received visitors; wrote his correspondence; and went to bed on a precise schedule that never varied." [23]

As leader of a religious school at Najaf, Khomeini continued to cultivate a following of students. Because of his presence, many students came to Najaf from Qom, his original base of teaching in Iran. They looked to him for guidance and leadership, not just in their personal lives but for all of Islam.

But Khomeini's attention constantly was on his homeland. He was apprised of the liberalization of Iranian culture—beaches where bikinis, not veils, had become women's standard dress; movie theaters that showed X-rated films; nightclubs where revelers danced provocatively. This was not the Iran of his youth. It was not the kind of society that had been encouraged by the prophet Muhammad.

Khomeini by this time had a vision for a new Iran. He had concluded that the shah himself was only one part of the country's problem. The entire system of government—a hereditary monarchy—was wrong, according to Islamic teaching. In taped and photocopied speeches that his devotees smuggled into Iran, he proclaimed that the Pahlavi reign must be brought to an end. In its place would emerge an Islamic republic, a government based on traditional Islamic teachings and similar to the seventh-century Islamic society of the prophet Muhammad and his followers. The ulema would be in charge of government.

Although he mainly campaigned for Islamic purity in his own country, Khomeini included his political and religious beliefs in a broad worldview. He taught that Muslim theologians bore responsibility for opposing all corrupt governments.

His tapes were played in mosques by religious leaders who agreed with him. Government agents cracked down on the subversive campaign. Mullahs thought to be enemies of the shah were placed under surveillance. Sometimes they were beaten or imprisoned. One was tortured to death. Meanwhile, the government took over some of Iran's mosques and Islamic schools, appointing clerics who did not oppose the shah.

Rather than force Khomeini's followers to cower, these severe actions brought the distant ayatollah new admirers. Notable among the mullahs who helped spread Khomeini's message throughout Iran were Muhammad Beheshti, Ali Khamenei, and Morteza Motahari. These men would help form the new Islamic government after the revolution.

During this period, one of the ayatollah's students taped and transcribed a series of his teacher's speeches. Published as a book, they would become perhaps Khomeini's most famous volume, *The Governance of the Jurist: Islamic Government* (*Velayet-e Faqih: Hukumat-e Eslami*). It naturally was outlawed by the Iranian government, but revolutionaries smuggled countless copies into the country. Many university students committed to memory—and to heart—statements made by Khomeini. They had found their voice, and they were ripe for revolution.

6

The Shah's Government Collapses

Late 1973 and 1974 was a boom time for members of the Organization of Petroleum Exporting Countries (OPEC). By forcing a hike in world oil prices, they multiplied their export profits to a wildly exorbitant level. In Iran, oil sales brought about $4 billion in 1973; it reached some $20 billion in 1974. While Western motorists waited in line at gas stations to pay inflated pump prices, OPEC leaders planned how they would spend their oil revenues.

Shah Pahlavi's government developed a long-term national improvement plan. It was projected to cost $70 billion over five years. Everyone was supposed to benefit: people on the street, businesses and industries, educational and military programs. The shah believed Iran could become one of the world's leading industrial powers by the end of the twentieth century.

Some Iranians indeed prospered. The Pahlavi family lived lavishly. So did those in business and administration who happened to be in strategic, oil-related positions. Journalist Mohamed Heikal, who covered events in the region before and after the Iranian revolution, wrote:

> The Shah was treating Iran as if it was his private property, and first pickings naturally went to his family. Certain unwritten boundaries were observed. The Queen Mother was only interested in real estate—land and buildings. . . . The Shah's brother, Prince Mahmud Reza, concentrated on mining. . . . Princess Ashraf was involved in banking, paper mills and lotteries, and so on. Loyal friends were not forgotten. General Zahedi's son, Ardeshir, who had married the Shah's daughter and been made ambassador in Washington, took over a controlling interest in the motor industry, and innumerable former politicians, diplomats, soldiers and businessmen were similarly rewarded, as were officials of the CIA who had proved helpful.[24]

Ayatollah Khomeini's fire of dissension for a time smoldered under general disinterest throughout Iranian society. In the end, though, reality did not come close to the shah's optimistic economic dream. Within two years, Iran was reeling under crushing inflation—40 percent annually. Iran did not have the skilled workforce to stoke industrial expansion. Foreigners had to be brought in, and they commanded higher salaries than Iranians, which worsened the inflation cycle. More than sixty thousand foreign industrial and military advisors and workers were in Iran by 1977.

Rather than a moneyed paradise, Iran quickly became a quagmire of problems. Khomeini was correct in his charges of corruption within the Pahlavi government. With a huge, oil-generated income to spend, some administrators used it wrongly, seeing to personal rather than national interests. People in many walks of life—scholars and laborers, educators and religious leaders, those in poverty and even some of the wealthy—became unhappy with the state of their nation. But they felt helpless.

Although Iran technically had a multiparty political system, the shah held firm control. Opposition groups were sharply divided. There was the National Front (NF), which had defied government assaults during the unrest of the early 1960s. But many university radicals scowled at the NF, deeming it too tame to bring about a revolution.

There was also the Communist party, Tudeh. It was not particularly popular in Iran, for the simple reason that atheistic communism does not fit in with Islamic fundamentalism. Nor did the Tudeh set well with Shah Pahlavi when it showed support toward Prime Minister Mosaddiq during the upheaval of the early 1950s. The Tudeh in time was largely subdued by the SAVAK, the government's secret security force.

Radical students organized political movements of their own and engaged not only in demonstrations but in urban terrorism. One organization that emerged in 1971 from a union of earlier groups was the Fedai-ye Khalq-e Iran. Its primary interest was not Islam but Marxism, in which communism is rooted. Another, organized in the mid-1960s, was the Mojahedin-e Khalq-e Iran. It began as a militant Islamic organization but in the mid-1970s splintered into two groups: Islam-oriented and socialist-oriented. Overall, it joined the many political entities opposing the Pahlavi regime.

In 1975, Shah Pahlavi established a single, uncontested party called Rastakhiz. This meant that, legally, no platform for orderly opposition to his regime was available.

Even so, the driving force behind the discontent was not political parties but the Shiite clergy. Other ayatollahs besides Khomeini wanted change and commanded great respect and sizable followings. Prominent among them was Ayatollah Muhammad Kazem Shariatmadari, who, like Khomeini, had taught at Borujerdi's school in Qom. Shariatmadari, far less aggressive than Khomeini, did not pursue actual revolution. He would remain withdrawn from Khomeini's denouncements and demands during the coming upheaval. In fact, he would express reservations about Khomeini's plan to have clerics control the government. Still, Khomeini owed him a debt of gratitude. Shariatmadari had joined other religious leaders in pleading for Khomeini's release from jail in the early 1960s.

Another leading cleric during the 1970s was Ayatollah Mahmoud Taleqani in the capital city. Much more like Khomeini than Shariatmadari, he actively opposed Pahlavi's regime and had been imprisoned for it. Taleqani lacked the broad base of followers that Khomeini was attracting. However, he would play a significant role in the shah's overthrow and in forging a new government. When he died of an apparent heart attack in September 1979, shortly after the revolution, some would suggest he was poisoned by Khomeini henchmen who feared Taleqani might contend for supreme control of the new republic.

In October 1977, an event occurred that devastated Khomeini personally and blew the antigovernment movement into a revolutionary fire. Khomeini's oldest son Mustafa died at an Islamic shrine in Karbala, Iraq. Like his father, grandfather, and great-grandfather before him, Mustafa was a Shiite cleric. He was forty-nine at the time. The cause of his death is not clear, but poisoning was widely rumored. Regardless of the actual circumstances, the ayatollah believed his son's death had been ordered by Shah Pahlavi and carried out by secret police.

Even if Khomeini's son had not died, revolution was in the air. Pahlavi tried to defuse it with concessions to the protesters. Pressured by U.S. President Jimmy Carter to adopt more liberal human rights policies, Pahlavi's regime freed several hundred political prisoners. The shah groped for other ways to make peace with his opponents. He took economic steps to counter inflation and made changes in his government.

It was all futile. When Pahlavi made a state visit to Washington, D.C., in late 1977, he was greeted by organized protesters. They had to be dispersed with teargas. The Carter administration apparently did not realize the deep trouble this suggested for the shah and for America because of its relations with him. In an embarrassingly famous statement made during a visit to Tehran at year's end, Carter told Shah Pahlavi, "Iran is an oasis of stability in a sea of trouble, and I am sure that the reason for this is the just, the great, and the inspired leadership of your majesty."[25]

In Iran, people who considered their government to be stable, just, great, or inspired were a dwindling minority. A clash of historic proportions was coming. Khomeini demanded that the Iranian military depose the shah and turn over control of the country to the people. Revolutionaries organized epic demonstrations. Protesters wielded posters and flags bearing the stern image of Khomeini.

What could the government do to quell the frenzy? In January 1978, *Eta'laat*, a government-controlled newspaper in Tehran, published an article severely attacking Khomeini politically and personally. It went so far as to suggest that he was a British agent, not the champion of Iranian nationalism he claimed to be. Khomeini's supporters responded with more marches and demonstrations in three dozen cities. Government troops put down the protests, sometimes with force. Several protesters were killed at Qom, where Khomeini, though long absent personally, now was a virtual idol to radical students. Later, more than a hundred died in Tabriz, where tanks were used to break up the mob.

Members of the ulema nourished the increasingly violent protests, calling on working-class opponents of the government to go on strike. Workers obeyed, demanding union powers and higher pay—and grinding Iran's economy to a near standstill. By late in the year, a broad segment of Iran's population opposed the government.

One of Khomeini's tactics for undermining the Pahlavi regime was to appeal to the military. Winning the sentiments of the soldiers eventually would be necessary, he knew. Although countless demonstrators were dying at the hands of the army, Khomeini did not condemn the men in uniform. Rather, in his taped messages he implored them not to harm the protesters, for they all were Muslims. Instead, he said, the army must turn against the godless shah and unite with the revolutionaries in a grand war on behalf of Allah.

His appeals clearly had an effect. By Autumn 1978, many soldiers were refusing to use force against demonstrators; some literally were joining the protesters on the spot. As we will see, soldiers deserted in legions as the revolution came to its climax. It would be perhaps the most incredible development of the revolution: One of the most modern armies on the planet, excellently equipped with Western weaponry purchased with oil money, was about to disintegrate.

Throngs of Iranians of different classes were convinced the Pahlavi government was evil. When more than four hundred people perished in a movie theater fire in Abadan in August 1978, suspicion immediately fell upon the SAVAK. The government, meanwhile, blamed Muslim extremists. One might wonder why the government would authorize a ghastly arson against theater-goers at a time when the regime's trustworthiness was under attack. The logic mattered little to rioters who took to the streets. The shah, they clamored, had to go.

In an attempt to control the situation, Pahlavi named Jafaar Sharif-Emami to serve as prime minister. The shah believed Sharif-Emami's close ties with religious leaders would quell the fire of revolution. Sharif-Emami proposed a "reconciliation" program to unite all classes of Iranians. He called for more political freedom, including the release of those jailed for political activities, a focus on human rights, and a campaign against government corruption.

From Iraq, the exiled Khomeini ignored the overtures. He tape-recorded anti-shah messages for distribution to his followers in Iran. The shah's regime must be overthrown, he exhorted. His message found a greater reception than that of Sharif-Emami.

THE WORLD MEETS A REVOLUTIONARY MASTERMIND

Until his rapid and dramatic rise to prominence in 1978, Ayatollah Khomeini was almost unknown outside the sphere of Iranian politics and religion. Many foreign journalists had never heard of Khomeini and did not know the meaning of the word *ayatollah*.

They were introduced to him during his brief stay outside Paris, as the revolution raced toward its climax. Former *Newsweek* writer Elaine Sciolino, in her book *Persian Mirrors*, recalled her first interview with the ayatollah—which was his first interview with either an American or a female journalist.

> I was told to take off my coat, cover my head, and take off my shoes, Persian style. . . . I was escorted into a small, unlit room, unfurnished except for rough tribal carpets that clashed with the garish pink-and-blue-flowered wallpaper. No independent interpreter or photographer was allowed.
>
> As I entered the room, Khomeini was already seated cross-legged on the floor, his hands folded in his lap, next to a fireplace and leaning against the wall. I was positioned a safe fifteen feet away. He didn't shake my hand. He didn't even stand to greet me. . . . During the forty-five-minute interview, Khomeini smiled only once, when his young grandson ran into the room and jumped into his lap, prompting the ayatollah to warmly embrace him.[*]

Not varying from his basic message of the past fifteen years, Khomeini raved to her against the shah's policies. His voice was mumbling and hardly understandable—but his message rang true to most Iranians.

* Source: Sciolino, pp. 50-51.

In early September, approximately a hundred thousand Khomeini supporters staged a march in Tehran. They demanded a new Islam-centered government with Khomeini in authority and the shah deposed. Martial law was ordered. Demonstrators on September 8, 1978, ignored the curfew (some may have been unaware of it) and assembled in Zhaleh Square. By certain accounts, militants among them rushed the soldiers who had been sent to control the situation; according to other versions of the story, soldiers started the violence by firing into the crowd. Whatever the case, the military resorted to using armored helicopters and tanks to break up the demonstration. The government said eighty-seven lives were lost; opponents said thousands were killed or injured. Khomeini's disciples labeled the day "Black Friday." To them, history was repeating itself after thirteen hundred years. The dead were proclaimed martyrs—like the followers of the ancient martyr Husain. They were slain by wicked government forces who allegedly represented the Muslim imposter Yezid.

The breach between the shah and his people could not be repaired. Even middle-class Iranians, while not inclined to protest in public, were losing confidence in the regime.

Still hoping to appease the opposition, Pahlavi purged government officials who were accused of abusing their power. Sharif-Emami was replaced as prime minister by General Gholam-Reza Azhari. The shah even withdrew from his governing role. He acknowledged that his regime had made mistakes and called on the opposition to give him a chance to implement reforms.

Meanwhile, his regime persuaded the Iraqi government to banish Khomeini from its country. Refused entry into neighboring Kuwait, Khomeini in October 1978 accepted an invitation of the Iranian Student Committee in Paris to relocate to France. The French government, not wishing to muddle Iran's internal politics, first asked the shah if Khomeini's residence in France would be acceptable. Believing the sheer distance would remove this revolutionary threat, Pahlavi consented.

Although Khomeini had not wanted to move so far away, the

decision turned out to be highly advantageous to his cause. Some of the largest newspapers and magazines in the world, including American periodicals, sent reporters to interview the man who was rousing such an intense public frenzy against an established government. During the four months he resided in the Paris suburb of Neauphle-le-Château, Khomeini granted an average of one interview a day. Now the whole world was reading about what had been, until then, merely a national crisis in an isolated Middle Eastern country. The attention of many millions was drawn to Iran.

Journalist and author Elaine Sciolino, at the time writing for *Newsweek*, described the scene in France:

> In those first few days, few supporters and almost no journalists visited Khomeini. Those supporters who did come brought along mattresses, rugs, sleeping bags, and even lawn chairs to make themselves comfortable. Some carried tape recorders to preserve the sermons or to send cassettes of them back home. . . .
>
> Khomeini said that the Shah must go. He said it over and over, to thousands of Iranian pilgrims who came to pay court and to hundreds of foreign journalists hungry like me for a story. He spoke in riddles, mumbled as he talked, and didn't smile. His followers lamented his situation—an exile, a transplanted Persian, having no access to a mosque. Eventually the Iranians rented a huge blue-and-white-striped tent, which they pitched on the lawn and called a mosque.[26]

Khomeini sent daily messages that were distributed by the thousands throughout Iran. The people heeded his call. Laborers in the oil industry—Iran's national lifeblood—went on strike within two weeks of Khomeini's arrival in France. Protesters disrupted banks, airlines, and Western-aligned businesses. In response, Shah Pahlavi appointed a military government to take over petroleum processing and to confront the radicals. This measure seemed to succeed momentarily, but by the end of the year, it was obvious to practically everyone that Iran's government was bound to change. Strikes had brought productive work in the country almost to a standstill. There were food shortages and power reductions. Ironically, the oil-rich country was forced to buy heating oil from the United States. Gasoline was in short supply, forcing automobile owners in Iran to wait in long lines. Gangs of young militants confiscated cars and stole the gas.

Once the shah's regime began to topple, it fell quickly. Despite the reported discontentment in Iran, most outsiders assumed that the government, backed by a large and sophisticated military machine, was secure. The events of 1978 and 1979, wrote political scientist Amin Saikal, "caught by surprise even most of those said to be best informed, including the CIA, for very few could foresee such a rapid collapse of the Shah's apparently well-entrenched and powerful administrative, security, and military apparatus." [27]

It finally became obvious even to the shah, who could not understand how matters had reached such a desperate crisis. Author William Shawcross in his book *The Shah's Last Ride* wrote:

> Until only months before, the Shah had genuinely believed that he was beloved by the Iranian people. Perhaps this meant no more than that he believed the propaganda, the lies, and the flattery of those who surrounded him; still, his belief had been complete. But in the last twelve months the fury of the entire nation had been aroused against him by an aged, exiled cleric for whom he had only contempt. Suddenly the people, his people, were expressing only loathing for all that he had achieved in his thirty-seven years on the throne. It was impossible for him to comprehend. [28]

By the end of 1978, relatives and intimates of the royal family were leaving Iran, taking what riches they could transport quickly. Luxuriant homes were left empty; soon they would be taken over by revolutionaries. The shah and his queen, Farah Diba, were urged by the U.S. ambassador in Tehran to leave as well. They began sending wardrobes and personal valuables by the planeload out of the country.

On January 16, 1979, Shah Pahlavi and his immediate entourage left the country, reputedly taking a vacation. Antigovernment militants rejoiced in the streets and toppled a public statue of the shah. They were confident he never would return—unless in custody, to stand trial for what they considered a long list of crimes against the people.

The shah left governmental control in the hands of a newly appointed prime minister, Dr. Shahpour Bakhtiar, a leader of the National Front. "Now you have everything in your hands," he told Baktiar at the Tehran airport before departing. "I hope you will succeed. I entrust Iran to you and to God."[29]

Bakhtiar, a reformer who was working to change the constitution, set up a Regency Council to oversee government affairs in the shah's absence. His efforts came far too late. Trying to allay the developing revolution was like trying to cap a volcano with a pot lid. Khomeini scoffed at the prime minister and his new council. He considered Bakhtiar illegitimate because he was controlled by the shah. Khomeini announced instead an Islamic Revolutionary Council and made plans to fly home to Iran in triumph.

Bakhtiar tried to prevent Khomeini's return, realizing the people needed only the presence of their legendary ayatollah for the revolution to explode. He ordered airports closed. But Bakhtiar's authority was evaporating. Khomeini arrived in Tehran from exile on February 1, 1979. He quickly signaled his intention to topple the shah's regime. Visiting a city cemetery where slain revolutionaries lay buried, he remarked acidly that "when we want to name a government, we get instead a cemetery full of people."[30]

For a dangerous week, civil war appeared imminent. While revolution-minded militants rampaged through Tehran, an army of four hundred thousand soldiers remained under the control of Bakhtiar's government. Fighting broke out between supporters of the revolution and loyalists to the shah. However, many troops soon began to defect to the cause of the revolution. Khomeini's new council named a prime minister of a transitional

Islamic government, Mehdi Bazargan. Bazargan was a religious leader who also had studied engineering. He was a long-time adversary of the shah.

As more members of the military joined Khomeini's legions,

THE SHAH'S PITIABLE DEMISE

What became of Shah Pahlavi, the man whose policies had provoked Khomeini's ire and led eventually to revolution?

In a very real sense, he became "homeless." After he left Iran, governments of other nations, including the United States, were more than a little uncomfortable with his presence. The shah was given a proper reception when his plane landed at Aswan, Egypt. He was invited by Egyptian President Anwar el-Sadat to stay as long as he wished. It was a tense respite, however. Pahlavi was distracted and uncertain of his standing, even among long-time allies. He was openly suspicious of the United States—as well he might have been. The Carter administration, realizing that the shah was in the throes of downfall, hoped to establish relations with Iran's revolutionary government. To the shah, this policy seemed to be an act of diplomatic deceit.

At the same time, the shah held a flicker of hope that Khomeini's revolution might falter. The Royal Guard in Iran might succeed in putting down the insurrection. Perhaps the ayatollah, despite his years of inflammatory talk, would be afraid to actually return to Iran and would remain in France—long enough, at least, for the fires of upheaval to die down.

After five days in Egypt, Pahlavi flew to Morocco. In the face of evermore hostile news from Iran, he quickly realized no foreign power really wanted him. Morocco, the Bahamas, and Mexico were only temporary residences. He finally was treated in the United States for what proved to be terminal cancer. He relocated briefly to Panama, then found asylum in his final months back in Egypt.

President Sadat had been Pahlavi's long-time friend. Sadat alone among international leaders braved the wrath of the Muslim world by giving Pahlavi a place to die peacefully. The end came for Pahlavi on July 27, 1980.

Sadat's sympathy for Pahlavi, coupled with a recent peace initiative with Israel, made fatal enemies for the Egyptian leader. He was assassinated in 1981.

Bakhtiar recognized the futility of resisting. After pro-Khomeini soldiers seized Iran's military bases and overpowered the loyal Imperial Guard, Bakhtiar disguised himself and fled for his life to Paris.

To the U.S. government, the actions of Iran's military were exasperating. The defectors were using American weapons to overthrow an American ally. During the early 1970s, when the United States considered the shah an anchor for American interests in the Middle East, it had sold a notable arsenal to the Iranian Army. Some of those weapons now were being used by a revolutionary force that soon would have American civilians in their sights.

In Iran, few observers during the period of chaos doubted the inevitable outcome. By February 11, it was all but over. Tehran Radio, then in the hands of revolutionaries, announced, "The dictatorship has come to an end."[31]

Middle East historian Roy Mottahedeh observed: "Khomeini had sat first in Iraq, then (after October 1978) in Paris, and said, 'The shah must go; the shah must go.' Other leading mullahs, including some of the 'models' in Qom, had been willing to compromise with the shah's government; but Khomeini had not. He spoke the word without compromise, and finally the shah left."[32]

Government under the shahs—the old Iran—was gone. Now, the world watched to see how a new regime rooted in Islamic fundamentalism would shape itself, and what life would be like for Iran's people in the decade of the 1980s.

7

Khomeini
in Power

In March 1979, Ayatollah Khomeini settled with his close advisors in Qom, the center of Islamic teaching where he had taught for many years before his exile. Local leaders from across the country journeyed to Qom to pay their respects to the ayatollah and declare their support. He greeted them, often with the cold, unsmiling demeanor that characterized him. Still, the significant thing was that he, unlike the shah, was accessible. Dilip Hiro reported that "he made himself available to ordinary Iranians who daily thronged to his unpretentious house, situated on a side street, in their hundreds. He received them in groups, listening to their problems and addressing them in return."[33]

But he had far more important concerns than meeting his public. He set about quickly defining the basis for the new Islamic Republic of Iran in no uncertain terms. He recognized the outlawed Palestine Liberation Organization (PLO) of Yasir Arafat and, as everyone expected, broke off all relations with Israel. Interestingly, he vowed to uphold the rights of the Jews—as many as thirty thousand—who lived in Iran.

Revolutionary forces had succeeded in uniting a majority of Iran's people to tumble Shah Pahlavi from power. Unity quickly evaporated, however, as their idealism settled into the reality of a nation fraught with problems. The factions and classes who had come together to oust the shah and force the return of the ayatollah were not of one mind. In fact, some—like the Tudeh Communists—were quite distant from Khomeini's Islamic-centered concept of government.

Khomeini's position was unique in history. A passionately popular religious leader returned from a long exile, he oversaw the revolution from a strange vantage point. He had effected a successful coup against his country's government, yet he was wholly unlike coup leaders in other troubled nations. They typically were military officers who, after wresting power, enjoyed a brief term as dictatorial head of state. Soon enough, they themselves were toppled—often in bloody fashion. Khomeini, by contrast, was no ambitious military man with a fleeting future. He was firmly fixed atop Iran's powerful Islamic religious establishment. He was not a primary political target, for he claimed no political title.

Indeed, he did not need one. As the supreme ayatollah, he was established in iron control of the country. Presidents and prime ministers of the new republic rapidly would come and go, just as they did in other countries rocked by revolution. Khomeini, on the other hand, would remain entrenched and removed from the political turmoil going on beneath him. He largely determined who would have key roles in government, including military commanders and judges. In many instances, he later gave his blessings to their opponents when he felt it was time for them to be replaced.

To the ulema, the objective all along had been an Islamic republic. Naturally, they felt they should be at the heart of power. Many young people, on the other hand, wanted a socialist state—Islamic in religion, but not primarily Islamic in operation. Others, meanwhile, favored a more liberal, Western-style system, one which was neither aligned with the United States nor controlled by the ulema.

While different groups theorized and opined, religious leaders set up a form of secret government. Courts sentenced members and supporters of the old regime to be executed—at least six hundred. The exiled shah himself was proclaimed a fugitive, to be put to death if he returned to the country.

Special targets of the early purge by revolutionaries were SAVAK agents. SAVAK, the shah's notorious security force organized in the aftermath of the 1950s Mosaddiq affair, was created specifically to sniff out and deal with conspirators against the government. It secretly probed opposition groups, notably Mosaddiq's National Front and the communistic Tudeh Party. Few were exempt from SAVAK scrutiny, however. Its agents even infiltrated Iranian radical organizations in foreign countries. It paid thousands of informers to spy on the activities and sentiments of the people around them. Anyone arrested by SAVAK was in dire jeopardy. Interrogators often used torture.

"Once a person fell into the arms of SAVAK there was nowhere to turn," wrote historian William Shawcross.

> SAVAK was empowered to act as the sole investigator of all alleged political crimes and also to bring charges. Suspects had no right to choose an independent lawyer, and usually were able to make contact with no one outside the prison. Once in SAVAK hands, people could simply disappear. . . . By the mid-seventies, fear of SAVAK extended even into the elite. Almost everyone with higher education knew someone who had disappeared, or whose death was thought, perhaps wrongly, to be the work of SAVAK. Even members of the [shah's] court were afraid.[34]

Members of the organization were well aware of their likely fate now that the shah's regime was gone. A few SAVAK operatives offered their services to the revolutionary government and were accepted. Most fled, or tried to. Those who were captured were doomed to quick execution—sometimes with, sometimes without, trials.

Who were the judges? By what authority did they condemn? This vendetta alarmed the more moderate ulema. No less an official than Bazargan, Khomeini's appointed prime minister, branded the political executions "a disgrace to the country and the revolution."[35]

An official vote on a form of government was held at the end of March 1979. Voters had but two choices: in favor of an Islamic republic or opposed to it. Ballots were of two colors: Green, signifying Islam, was a pro vote; red, signifying the ancient tyrant Yezid, was a no vote. In light of the previous year's events, few voters were likely to oppose the ayatollah's intended form of government. Khomeini won his referendum and proclaimed Iran to be an Islamic republic.

Although Khomeini could claim an overwhelming mandate in the referendum, many revolutionary groups, ethnic groups, and even religious leaders and officials in the new government were unhappy with it. They had hoped voters would have more than two stark options when choosing their new form of government.

Kurds and certain other minority groups refused to participate in the voting.

Later that year, a national referendum approved a new constitution to replace the one of 1906. It retained the Majlis, the elected parliament, and provided for a president to be elected by popular vote. The president, in turn, would appoint a prime minister and cabinet (subject to Majlis approval) to actually run the government.

What, officially, would be the ayatollah's role in the new Iran? American journalist Elaine Sciolino had asked him that question during his exile in France. His response: "I will not have any position in the future government. I will not be the President or the Prime Minister. I will be some sort of supervisor of their activities. I will give them guidance. If I see some deviation or mistake, I will remind them how to correct it."[36]

Khomeini made himself *valayate-faqih*, a term which implied legal authority behind his total control of the government. Khomeini could name the country's president and oversee all branches of government: presidential, judicial, and legislative. This was unprecedented and dangerous power, in the minds of many leaders. Ayatollah Shariatmadari, for one, protested that this title of absolute authority was not necessarily established by Islamic law. Prime Minister Bazargan, for another, worried that Iran in effect was replacing one monarch—the deposed shah—with another.

Historian Elton L. Daniel observed that the new constitution generally "sought to completely Islamize the state in accordance with the ideas of the architect of the revolution, the Ayatollah Ruhollah Khomeini."[37]

Besides the countless executions, the action that brought world criticism upon Khomeini's new regime was his campaign against people he considered morally undesirable, including prostitutes and homosexuals. At the same time, he turned back the clock to the time before Iran had become "Westernized." Strict Islamic codes of dress and behavior were enforced. Alcoholic drinks were forbidden, women were required to cover their heads in public, and Western entertainment was banned.

American journalist Robin Wright, in her book *The Last Great Revolution*, contrasted visits she made to Iran in 1973, at the height of the shah's regime, and shortly after the revolution. "Iran was then an openly inviting place for an American woman," she wrote of her first trip. "I felt as relaxed about traveling throughout the country as I did in Europe. I could go most places, do virtually anything, talk to anyone and dress in whatever apparel I chose. Short skirts were acceptable." Less than a decade later, she was introduced to a very different lifestyle before her plane even touched down at the airport: "Before we landed in Tehran, the flight's lone stewardess helped me tighten a big headscarf and button up a baggy ankle-length coat known as a *roopoosh* to better cover my hair and neck. She also gave me ten Band-Aids to cover the nail polish I'd forgotten to remove."[38] At the airport, among Wright's personal belongings seized and ritually destroyed by customs officials was her deck of playing cards.

As for Iran's own news media, it was brought under tight government control. Any statements Khomeini and his followers considered critical or even questionable were censored.

Such measures alarmed many Iranians. They had supported Khomeini in deposing the shah, but they did not realize his new government would rule with such a heavy hand. Khomeini himself stated that the brand of political suppression practiced by the Pahlavi regime was unacceptable. "Our people have been in prison for 35 years; no government is going to put them in prison again," the ayatollah proclaimed. "They must be given a chance to express themselves as they wish, even if it means a certain degree of chaos."[39]

Violent opposition groups launched a reign of terror, assassinating some of the ayatollah's lieutenants. Government forces brutally put down the resistance. They also dealt violently with rebellious Kurds and other ethnic groups.

In November 1979, radicals turned their revolution into a major international event. Some four hundred militant young Iranians seized the sprawling U.S. Embassy compound in Tehran. It was their second attempt to do so; a violent attack earlier that year had been thwarted when the revolutionary government sent a rescue force to the embassy. This time, fifty-two American hostages were taken. Thus began a crisis between the two countries that would last over a year. It is unclear whether Khomeini knew of the embassy attack beforehand, but he clearly condoned it. He was deeply angered when U.S. President Carter allowed Shah Pahlavi to seek medical treatment in America. Khomeini, who would come to brand the United States as "the Great Satan,"[40] demanded that the former shah be returned to Iran to stand trial. Khomeini complimented the students who took control of the American Embassy—one of whom was his son Ahmad.

Prime Minister Bazargan, who had been trying to establish a

HATRED AND HOSTAGES

The election year of 1980 was a somber one in the United States. Americans watched news images of gaunt prisoners, often bound and blindfolded—former occupants of the U.S. embassy in Tehran now held hostage by Iranian militants. Hopes repeatedly were dashed as hints of their pending release came to nothing. The tragic failure of a military rescue mission in April triggered humiliation and rage.

For most Americans, this was their introduction to Ayatollah Khomeini, Iran's new leader. His frowning, intimidating picture was fixed permanently in the minds of an entire generation. As they saw it, he clearly had the power to free the prisoners, but he did nothing. With Khomeini's obvious approval, the victims had been taken at gunpoint from a place internationally recognized as a haven of safety. To Americans, this ayatollah could not possibly be a true man of God. They came to detest him at least as fervently as he detested the U.S. government.

Many political historians believe the fifteen-month hostage crisis was the main reason President Jimmy Carter lost his reelection bid. The prisoners were released in January 1981 as Carter's successor, President Ronald Reagan, was being inaugurated. Khomeini had effected a leadership change in not one country, but two.

For many Americans a quarter century later, the hostage crisis is unforgettable. At the mention of Iran or Ayatollah Khomeini, they call to mind blindfolded prisoners and a frightful, glowering man in a black turban.

tentative relationship with the United States, failed to get the hostages released. He resigned two days after the embassy takeover. Bazargan was replaced, unofficially, by Ayatollah Muhammad Beheshti, secretary of the new Revolutionary Council and a former student of Khomeini's.

Abolhassan Bani-Sadr, the candidate favored by Khomeini, easily won election to the presidency in January 1980, becoming Iran's first president after the revolution. Bani-Sadr had been the leader of the Iranian Student Committee in Paris who had asked Khomeini to move there from Iraq in the autumn of 1978. However, he hoped for a more moderate Islamic republic than the one being pressed by Khomeini's radical supporters. Bani-Sadr found Khomeini's position and plans for the country quite unstable. In the Majlis elections in the spring of 1980, voters gave majority control of the fundamentalist ulema to the Islamic Republican Party (IRP). These were rivals of Bani-Sadr and his liberal supporters. One of the IRP party leaders, Muhammad Ali Rajai, was named prime minister.

Meanwhile, the upheaval in Iran had created a crisis abroad. Negotiations to release the American Embassy hostages stalled, pressuring President Carter to take military action. He approved a daring rescue mission in April 1980. Six huge transport planes and eight U.S. Navy helicopters rendezvoused at an isolated desert landing strip several hundred miles from Tehran. From there, they planned to launch a night raid. The rescue attempt turned out to be a tragic, humiliating disaster. In a sandstorm, a helicopter and plane collided. Three other helicopters were badly damaged. Eight U.S. soldiers were killed, and the rescue team returned empty-handed. They had come nowhere near their objective.

The rescue attempt provoked a new frenzy among Iranian radicals to purge military and civil officials suspected of being sympathetic to the deposed shah. Approximately eight thousand officials were dismissed; some were executed.

An even greater drama was soon to come. In late September 1980, President Saddam Hussein of neighboring Iraq launched an invasion into Iran. Hussein had several reasons for going to war. First, he—like other Middle Eastern leaders—feared that Khomeini's legions were working to spread their revolution all across the Islamic world. Second, he knew that Khomeini considered him an enemy of the first order. The ayatollah despised Hussein's policies and his Baath Party, which he called "infidel."[41] Khomeini despised Hussein personally because Hussein was a Sunni Muslim, a traditional rival of the Shiites. Hussein believed his forces easily could conquer an Iranian military that was weakened by the revolution. If successful, he could demand key territory in the border region and, he hoped, rise to prominence among leaders of the Middle East.

It may seem odd that Khomeini would bear such loathing for a neighboring country that had been his home in exile from the mid-1960s until 1978. However, the Iraqi government had not been a particularly gracious host. It had ordered Khomeini's arrest more than once and had ultimately expelled him from Iraq.

Moreover, as the foremost Shiite leader, Khomeini had no more respect for Hussein than he had for the deposed shah. Hussein came to power in 1980, the year after Khomeini returned to establish Iran's Islamic Republic. Hussein's Baath political party, which had been formed in Syria in 1953, was rooted in socialism. It had certain basic objectives in common with those of Khomeini: notably, a united Islamic world, independent of outside influences. What it mainly lacked, though, was Khomeini's fiery insistence on Islamic influence in government. To Baathists, Islamic teaching is a secondary interest; the destruction of Israel and Muslim unity in a Marxist-style utopia are primary. Khomeini went so far as to call Hussein and the Baath Party "anti-Islamic."[42] He urged Iraq's majority Shiite population to rise up in revolution, as his followers had done in Iran. Understandably, Hussein decided it would be in his best interest to wreck Iran's dangerous new regime, or at least neutralize it.

The invasion initially went well for Iraq. Its forces occupied some ten thousand square miles of territory in Iran, including the major port of Khorramshahr at the border and important oil fields in Iran's Khuzistan region. The Iranians' military command structure was in disarray during the revolution and hardly able to counter Hussein's forces. Indeed, many of its senior officers had been executed, accused of loyalty to the deposed shah.

Iran soon managed to halt the Iraqi thrust, however. It did so with what was in large part a curious people's army—masses of untrained militia willing to die for their new republic. The war would continue for years, with neither country gaining a decisive edge.

President Bani-Sadr was not destined to lead the Islamic Republic of Iran for long. He curried the support of the Mujahedeen-e-Khalq, political challengers of the controlling IRP. In June 1981 in response, the IRP voted to oust Bani-Sadr from the presidency. Khomeini, the president's old mentor and idol, approved the ouster. Bani-Sadr went to France in exile.

In response to being stripped of their political prestige, the Mujahedeen launched a guerrilla war against the government. They were a formidable faction, with some ten thousand followers in the Tehran area. But they faced a formidable enemy: the Revolutionary Guard, which had been created to ensure by force that the new Iran kept to the purposes of the revolution.

When a bomb devastated IRP headquarters in June 1981, the IRP-controlled government blamed Mujahedeen terrorists—although a French terrorist organization claimed responsibility for the act. More than seventy people died in the attack. They included Ayatollah Beheshti, one of the highest government leaders, and some forty other government officials.

Regardless of who really was behind the bombing, the Mujahedeen clearly was bent on violence in its antigovernment campaign. A bomb blast at a government meeting August 30 claimed the lives of President Muhammad Ali Rajai and Prime Minister Muhammad Javad Bahonar. Both men had only recently taken office. Some twelve hundred political and religious leaders had died at the hands of Mujahedeen militants by early 1982, according to estimates.

Vengeance was far more vicious. Government forces, at Khomeini's bidding, captured and killed some four thousand members of the Mujahedeen, including ten who held government positions. This massive vendetta effectively crushed the opposition party, although the Mujahedeen continued operations on a minor scale. Other political parties, including the leftist Tudeh, also suffered repression. The more moderate Islamic People's Republican Party, established by Ayatollah Shariatmadari and his followers in 1979, was disbanded and some of its leaders killed. As we will see, the days were numbered for Shariatmadari himself. Reviewing the situation in the mid-1980s, author Said Amir Arjomand wrote, "In sum, since their direct seizure of power in November 1979, the militant ayatollahs have ruthlessly dealt with all its organized political opponents, and have by and large succeeded in destroying them."[43]

At the same time, Iran was turning the tide against the Iraqi invaders. Hordes of Iranians—many of them young civilians or religious leaders believing themselves to be martyrs in the service of the ayatollah—threw themselves into a bloody counterattack. They drove back the occupation forces and reclaimed most of their lost territory.

Just as importantly, Iran's economy was beginning to stabilize after two years of breakdown. Three million working-class Iranians had been unemployed, skilled laborers and managers had fled the chaos, inflation had spiraled, and food shortages had been devastating. Now things were improving. The economic base, as before the revolution, was the sale of oil.

Not so stabilized, on the other hand, was the political situation. A high-ranking official and former aide to Khomeini, Sadiq Qotbzadeh, was accused of joining a coup attempt in April 1982. Qotbzadeh, seventy military officers, and about a hundred others were arrested and put to death. Although his involvement in the plot was questionable (he denied the accusation), Qotbzadeh in fact had come to oppose Khomeini's new government. A letter written shortly before his execution revealed his remorse at having supported "the satanic regime of the mullahs."[44] Qotbzadeh and Bani-Sadr had urged an early end to the American hostage crisis, in contrast to the IRP leadership.

With the quelling of this revolt, the religious leaders who followed Khomeini were in virtually total control of the new government. But they were by no means in agreement over how the country should function. Author James Haskins surmised: "The mullahs disagreed on so many things that they left the average Iranian in a state of fear and confusion. The various revolutionary guards and committees that made up the ruling structure acted quite independently of each other."[45]

In general, the ruling committees sought to reveal crimes against Islamic teachings and to punish the perpetrators. Paranoia became the norm in Iranian society. Citizens were encouraged to spy on one another and report wrongful actions or attitudes. Naturally, some of their accusations were unproven, if not deliberately falsified. Teachers became suspicious of their students, for even small children were engaged to report on adults.

Morale in Iranian society plummeted. People faced uncertainty, not just for the future but from day by day. The outside world looked aghast at a country that seemed to have come under the thumb of a merciless religious fanatic. Many Iranians reached the same sobering conclusion. Yet, their ayatollah was the leader they had clamored for in their zeal to bring down the Pahlavi dynasty.

By the end of 1982, even the ayatollah himself realized that the Islamic Republic he had created was too repressive against its own people to succeed. In a risky but necessary concession, he proclaimed sweeping reforms of the government system. Citizens' privacy, he announced, was to be protected. In fact, people were allowed to wage complaints against government brutality. The rampant personal spying he originally had encouraged among neighbors, families, and students was now considered a crime.

But was his new policy to be entirely trusted? If someone lodged a complaint alleging mistreatment by a government agent or committee, might they be arrested or abused, even executed, if the leadership later returned to its harsh stance? The decade of the 1980s for Iranians was one of unprecedented insecurity and fear.

8

A Troubled Decade

During its first decade as an Islamic republic, Iran experienced complex changes. Some had little to do with the revolution. For example, the population was becoming increasingly urban. This trend had begun years before, as thousands of farmers and villagers, facing unrelieved hardships in their rural lifestyles, began moving to cities in quest of better conditions. It was hardly an improvement; many of the newcomers found themselves living in deplorable shantytowns. Their plight was worsened by overpopulation—a social trend that Khomeini encouraged. Iran's population mushroomed from fewer than 40 million when Khomeini assumed power to almost 70 million in mid-2003. Naturally, the average age of Iranians is low; approximately half are younger than twenty.

At the same time, many rural peasants found opportunities in the tumultuous aftermath of the revolution. They literally seized control of much of the land from its original owners. The revolutionary government was indecisive in dealing with the resulting violence. After the Majlis in 1980 passed a property redistribution measure, religious leaders—including Khomeini—questioned its legality according to Qur'anic doctrine. They had parts of the land law nullified. Local revolutionary committees, or *komitehs*, assumed authority over many farming operations.

Khomeini's ideal of a Muslim-run, nationalistic government system was defined only vaguely. The new leader was a theorist, not a practical administrator. This had been obvious to reporter Elaine Sciolino, one of the journalists who interviewed him in France shortly before his return to Iran. Khomeini, she later wrote, "didn't have a master plan for the future. Rather, with the help of his aides, he improvised. Day by day, ideas were formulated, assignments were given, committees were appointed. His answers about what his government might look like evaporated into an Islamic mist as he called himself the symbol of the people."[46]

To confuse matters further, Khomeini sometimes reversed himself. In late 1983, he stated publicly that he was not above making mistakes. "I may have said something yesterday, changed it today, and will again change it tomorrow."[47] Author Daniel

Brumberg, in his book *Reinventing Khomeini: The Struggle for Reform in Iran*, commented, "Such vacillating hardly fit the image of the 'True Believer' that Khomeini's disciples associated with the Imam, leader of the Muslim community. How could the 'Shadow of God' admit that he had 'made a mistake'?"[48]

It mattered little, in terms of his popularity. Iranians still held him in awe. From his vantage point as Iran's guiding light, Khomeini deferred hands-on problem solving to subordinates. For the struggling new republic, this resulted in near calamity. While there is wisdom in delegating authority, in this situation it posed a dilemma of strangling proportions. Since his underlings did not always agree among themselves as to specific steps to take, the effectiveness of the new government was seriously impaired.

Policies turned especially murky when faced with the realities of the economy. Radical leaders brought industries, banks, and insurance firms under the control of the state. However, many within the new government argued that a measure of free enterprise would be necessary in order for the system to work. Their disagreement went unresolved. When Khomeini died in 1989, confusion remained in the regime's economic strategies.

He was an unquestioned hero to the underprivileged, nonetheless. Historian Nikki R. Keddie, in his book *Roots of Revolution* published shortly after Khomeini came to power, observed that the ayatollah "continually associates himself with the needs of the poor or 'dispossessed' and has taken steps to implement this identification, which adds to his popularity."[49] That popularity remained hardly diminished at his death, judging from the millions of distraught Iranians who would throng to Tehran for his funeral.

Journalist and author Mohamed Heikal, in his 1981 work *Iran: The Untold Story*, provided a quaint glimpse of the home life of Iran's new leader:

> It is still Khadijah [Khomeini's wife] who cooks the Ayatollah's food for him. His routine is regular and his menu simple. He wakes at about 5 a.m. for the dawn prayer, then goes back to

sleep again. His breakfast, consisting of bread and a saucer of honey, is placed by Khadijah for him beside his *doshak* [floor blanket]. At 11 a.m. he has a little fruit juice, usually orange juice, and at noon a little rice and boiled meat, which he eats with a spoon—the only utensil he ever uses. He is particularly fond of the yellow Persian water-melons. After his midday meal he has a nap, then wakes for the afternoon prayer and continues dealing with business and meeting people until after midnight. Khomeini does not smoke, and never uses the telephone, though while he was in France he once made an exception to this rule when he heard that his brother, Basandidah, was very ill and he wished to hear his voice. The elder brother now occupies the small house in a side street which used to be the Ayatollah's home until he attained power. Now he has moved to a new residence, one of a group of four houses, all single-storey, grouped on either side of a street. One pair contains the offices of his secretary and personal mullah, his security guards, and so on. Across the street one house contains a section of revolutionary guards and the other is the Ayatollah's own home. Inside there is a reception room, about 16 feet by 24, with an undistinguished blue carpet on the floor and spotlights cluttering the ceiling. It looks like a makeshift television studio. This leads into three tiny private rooms and a minute kitchen. One of these rooms is for Khomeini's wife, one for any member of the family who wishes to make use of it, and the final one is Khomeini's own bedroom. From what I could see, all his worldly possessions there consisted of his *doshak* and a trunk containing his clothes.[50]

Dilip Hiro, in *Iran Under the Ayatollahs* (1985), noted, "Khomeini is a man of regular habits. He leads an orderly life, and is known for his serenity. He never leaves his premises and seldom, if ever, uses the phone."[51]

It was by no means a serene period for the people of Iran. They were adapting to a new state marked by stern Shiite demands in their daily life. "Through law and intimidation," wrote historian

Sandra Mackey, "the mandate of hejah wrapped every woman, Muslim and non-Muslim, in layers of dark clothing, and strict sexual segregation descended on the whole society from schools to parks to the beaches of the Caspian Sea."[52]

Iranian art and media were placed under new controls. "The themes of love and eroticism, present for centuries in Persian poetry, disappeared, replaced by verbal images of religion and revolution," Mackey wrote. "The same applied to prose and to painting. In the filmmaking industry, controls clamped on by the Office of Islamic Guidance slashed production in 1981 to only seven movies, which were all made in one genre—the heroic Muslim male standing firm against corruption and injustice in the name of the revolution."[53] Universities throughout the country were closed for more than two years while censors purged them of unholy textbooks and allegedly misguided faculty.

Damaging effects of the revolution would continue to hamper the film industry when, years later, cinema again became widely available to the public. During the revolution, terrorists had targeted theaters as symbols of Western intrusion. Approximately half of Iran's movie houses had been destroyed or taken over by the clergy.

Meanwhile, the country was mired in its war with Iraq. By 1988, more than a million lives had been lost—three-fourths of them Iranians. The Iraqi Army, with support from other countries that their President Hussein had arranged, possessed better weapons. Iran, however, had several times the population of Iraq. Numbers alone weighed heavily in the outcome. Gradually, Iran reclaimed all its lost territory and even went on the offensive, striking targets on Iraqi soil. Hussein, realizing his hopes for supremacy in the region were lost, made overtures for peace with Iran.

Khomeini was of no mind for compromise. He laid down extreme conditions for peace—billions of dollars to repay Iran for war losses. These included oil industry and farming disruptions and the destruction of more than a thousand Iranian villages, towns, and cities. Khomeini even demanded that Hussein's regime be terminated in the name of Islam. He knew that apart from the human cost, the war had turned out to be more ruinous to Iraq than to Iran. Iraq, oil-rich before the 1980 invasion, within eight years found itself some $40 billion in debt to foreign nations, largely as a result of its military spending and war-related losses.

However, Khomeini's radical demands and his fighters' willingness to die martyrs' deaths were countered chillingly by Hussein's sheer ruthlessness. Hussein ordered the use of chemical weapons—not just against Iranians but, when necessary, against his own people. Late in the war, after Iranian forces captured the Iraqi town of Halabja, Hussein had the town bombed with poison gas. Among the casualties were, according to some estimates, more than five thousand Iraqi civilians.

It became obvious to the Iranian regime that while Hussein was failing in his bid to conquer them, he would stop at nothing to avert defeat. Stalemate, in the end, would be the wise solution. A cease-fire finally was arranged in the summer of 1988. It had been one of the longest and most deadly conflicts in modern Middle Eastern history.

The effect of the overall turmoil on the Iranian people was incalculable. Historian Roy Mottahedeh, in his 1985 book *The Mantle of the Prophet*, wrote:

> In the past five years, as Iran has moved through a political and cultural revolution with dramatic and often violent aftermaths and entered a long and bitter war with its neighbor Iraq, many thousands of Iranians have been executed, tens of thousands have died in battle, and hundreds of thousands have chosen to live in exile. Any consensus on the meaning of the Iranian past has been torn up by the deeply felt disagreement among Iranians over the meaning of the Iranian present.[54]

Throughout this period, Iran's leadership functioned under a strange method of operations, by most definitions of government. In every matter, Khomeini was the ultimate decision-maker—yet, he was in weakening health and literally overwhelmed by the issues brought to his attention. Quoting from Heikal's 1981 book:

> It became impossible for him to concentrate for more than twenty minutes at a time. Although all important questions continue to come to him for decision, his reactions are instinctive rather than thought out. He reads no reports. In the early days after his return to Qom he used to complain that every day he was being sent three reports—one from the Foreign Ministry about foreign security, one about internal affairs, and one on economic matters. He begged the officials in Tehran to stop sending them. "I never read them," he said.

CHESS—A SMALL VICTORY OVER REPRESSION

In the immediate aftermath of the revolution, Shiite hard-liners imposed stringent Islamic values and demands on every facet of Iranian society. Colleges were closed and the film industry virtually suspended while officials determined which elements of literature and arts must be eliminated and which would be permissible in the new Islamic republic.

One curious victim of the zealous and often violent national purge was the ancient game of chess. It was banned in Iran in 1981 because some players and audiences were using it as a gambling device—and because Ayatollah Khomeini believed chess caused brain damage. Iranian enthusiasts of the game defied the edict, continuing to compete in secret. In 1988, after deciding chess was actually a good mental exercise, Khomeini lifted the ban. He insisted, however, that it must not interfere with daily prayers and must not involve gambling.

It was neither the first nor last time that chess was outlawed in the region. An early caliph shortly after the prophet Muhammad's death declared the game offensive to Islamic teaching because carved images—idols—were used for chess pieces. In 1996, eight years after Khomeini lifted the ban in Iran, the Taliban regime in neighboring Afghanistan forbade the game and jailed chess players. They, like the Iranian clergy before them, cited chess as a distraction from Islam and a method of gambling. The ban remained in place until the Taliban leadership was overthrown five years later.

> In Qom there is no formal method of conducting business. The direct, personal relationship which Khomeini has maintained with the masses has rendered abortive all attempts at creating some sort of real political life in Iran. Every morning his supporters come to him from all over Iran, in buses, taxis, any way they can manage. He greets them from the roof of his house, and has a brief dialogue with their leader. . . .[55]

Khomeini's headquarters were heavily guarded by revolutionaries. Visitors had to submit to a series of body searches and hand over all personal items, even keys and rings, before they were admitted into the ayatollah's presence. A sophisticated security system covered the yards and buildings. Antiaircraft guns surrounded the compound. Defense personnel had orders to shoot down any aircraft in the area.

On the minds of everyone was an uncertain future. What would become of the nation and its government after the death of Khomeini, who was now in his eighties and suffering from heart disease? Who could possibly replace him? The ayatollah, after all, was a mere mortal despite his iron grip on Iran. His health became a subject of speculation immediately after the revolution. After 1982, he rarely made public appearances. People openly wondered why. Did he consider it beneath his dignity? Or was he physically unable to move about freely?

In 1985, a panel known as the Council of Experts proposed that Ayatollah Husein Ali Montazeri be named heir to Khomeini's role. Montazeri, already in his sixties, had been a close follower of Khomeini through the years of upheaval. He was considered somewhat more moderate than his teacher, more willing to compromise. Nevertheless, he clearly followed the ayatollah's political views and had become a principal leader of the ulema.

As it turned out, Montazeri became critical of the new government. Because of this, he fell from favor. In 1989, just months before Khomeini's death, he was stripped of his authority.

The Islamic Republic of Iran maintained its animosity toward the United States, not just because the United States had supported Shah Pahlavi's regime but because it supported Israel. Khomeini was among the more militant Middle Eastern leaders opposing Israel. "We shall soon liberate Jerusalem and pray there," he proclaimed to his people.[56] In 1982, Iran sent troops to Lebanon, Israel's northern neighbor, to help secure that country. When the U.S. Embassy in Beirut, Lebanon, and other Western targets were bombed in 1982 and 1983, Iranian operatives were suspected to be behind the attacks.

Journalist Mohamed Heikal noted that Khomeini had a "profound conviction that from the beginning the Jews have hated Islam and have tried to frustrate it. When the state of Israel was founded Khomeini immediately denounced it."[57]

While he opposed the United States and Israel, however, Khomeini refused to turn to the former Soviet Union as a super-power ally. For one thing, the Soviets had aided Iraq during the 1980s war. For another, the Soviets' communistic government denied the existence of God and repressed Muslims as well as believers of other faiths. With Islam at its heart, the new Iran was hardly likely to forge close ties with an atheistic nation.

Iranian hostility toward the Soviets dated to the nineteenth century. Wars had been fought between Russia and Persia. During the late 1800s and early 1900s, the shah had granted trade privileges to Russian merchants. Russia had even annexed territory in the border region between the two empires. When the Bolsheviks (Communists) rose to power in Russia in 1917, they sent an army to Tehran to bully and subdue the shah.

While the Soviets intimidated many peoples and countries during the twentieth century, Khomeini brazenly snubbed them in defining Iran's international stance. "The Soviet Union," he said, "can do nothing. It has proved it is capable of nothing."[58]

Other governments in the region, meanwhile, viewed the new Iran with growing wariness and distrust. Some of Khomeini's lieutenants openly suggested that their leader be recognized as the leader of all Shiite Muslims. The ayatollah himself branded the government of Saudi Arabia as an unworthy steward of Mecca, Islam's holy city. Wrote historian William C. Cleveland:

"The emergence in Iran of a militant Islamic Republic caused tremors among conservative monarchs and reformist dictators alike, and Iran became isolated in the Middle East."[59] Even Arafat's Palestine Liberation Organization, which won Khomeini's support after the revolution, became concerned with the ayatollah's vision for crushing Israel and taking over Jerusalem, the city at the heart of Israeli-Arab tensions. The PLO long had sought an independent Palestine along the River Jordan, with Jerusalem as its capital. It feared that Khomeini had other plans for the ancient holy city.

No one, regardless of how powerful, was truly secure during the years of Khomeini's leadership. Many of the best-educated and most-skilled citizens, troubled by the actions of the new regime, quietly departed the country. They left a void that was difficult to fill. Even prominent Muslim clerics were held suspect by the government if they showed less than enthusiastic support for Khomeini and his lieutenants.

A tragic example was Ayatollah Shariatmadari. He was a man who scorned politics but who had helped dissuade the shah's government from placing Khomeini on trial and possibly executing him in the 1960s. Shariatmadari voiced support for the Iranian revolution but opposed violence. He also questioned the wisdom of having a Muslim-run government. He thus became a target of the radical leadership.

When the government in April 1982 arrested some two hundred people in the Qotbzadeh conspiracy plot against Khomeini's regime, Shariatmadari was implicated. Khomeini's henchmen built a case that Shariatmadari had known of the alleged plot and refused to divulge it to authorities. They also produced documents (of questionable veracity, according to some historians) that suggested close ties between Shariatmadari, Shah Pahlavi, and U.S. interests. They were afraid of dangerous protests if they executed an ayatollah of Shariatmadari's stature, so they stripped him of his authority and placed him under house arrest. Aging and feeble, he died in 1985. Some believe he had been deprived of adequate medical care.

While Khomeini over the years cited many alien doctrines as enemies of Islam, he was not above appealing to their followers. An example was the Christmas message he addressed to the American people in December 1979, during the hostage crisis. The Iranian Embassy in Washington wanted to have the ayatollah's letter published in *The Washington Post* (which refused). For years, Khomeini had denounced the United States and considered Christianity and Zionism to be wayward, anti-Islamic beliefs. Yet, in his Christmas message to Americans, he paid remarkable tribute to Jesus. Khomeini called on America to return the exiled shah to Iran to face judgment. His text was directed specifically to Christian readers. Khomeini quoted from Jesus's Beatitudes ("Blessed are those who hunger and thirst for justice. . . ."). He acknowledged Jesus as "the spirit of God" and "a great messenger whose mission was to establish justice and mercy, and who with his heavenly words and deeds condemned the tyrants and supported the oppressed."[60]

Although he was quoting from the Bible, to the end of his life, Khomeini demanded total respect for the Qur'an. His insistence reached an alarming extreme only months before his death. A British author named Salman Rushdie—himself a Muslim born in India—wrote a novel titled *The Satanic Verses*, published in September 1988. It won scant acclaim as a work of literature, but it became one of the best-known books of the decade. This was because many Muslims, including the ayatollah, considered part of it to be an obscene mockery of the prophet Muhammad. In February 1979, Khomeini proclaimed that "the author of *The Satanic Verses*, which is against Islam, the Prophet, and the Koran, and all those involved in its publication who were aware of its content, are sentenced to death."[61]

The Muslim world heeded the call. A frenzy of public protests were organized to condemn Rushdie and, in the process, to condemn Great Britain and the United States. Islamic organizations offered rewards totaling $6 million for the killing of Rushdie, forcing the author to go into hiding. The Iranian government severed diplomatic relations with Great Britain.

The Rushdie episode showed the ayatollah not just as an extraordinarily militant Muslim leader, but as one seemingly gripped by religious paranoia. *The Satanic Verses*, he told other clerics, was part of a broad effort by Israel and Western countries to "annihilate Islam."[62]

Perhaps he really believed it. Some have conjectured, though, that the death sentence against Rushdie was a public relations ploy. They suggested that Khomeini took this opportunity to portray himself worldwide as the foremost defender of his faith. He still hoped the revolution he had ignited might spread to other Islamic countries.

But almost no time remained for Iran's peerless leader. Little had been seen of him in public during his declining years. How much longer would the ayatollah be with his people? Even as fanatical assassins searched the globe for Salman Rushdie, that question was on the minds of many both inside and outside Iran.

Death came by heart attack on June 3, 1989, after the ayatollah underwent intestinal surgery. Tehran Radio somberly proclaimed, "The lofty spirit of the leader of the Muslims and the leader of the noble ones, His Eminence Imam Khomeini, has reached the highest status, and a heart replete with love and God and his true people, who have endured numerous hardships, has stopped beating."[63]

A decade later, historians who scrutinized Iran's revolutionary experience on the whole were less reverent. Khomeini died "a broken man after Iran's failure to defeat Iraq in eight years of war," wrote Geneive Abdo in *Answering Only to God*, "but his theological and political legacies continue to dominate the country."[64]

Iranians sent him to his grave with the same hysterical idolization they had shown when he arrived in Tehran from exile. Ignoring a wilting summer heat wave, millions from across the nation converged on Tehran to pay their respects as his corpse lay in state. During his funeral procession, mourners rushed the open casket to tear off fragments of his white burial cloth. As in the days of revolution, soldiers had to fight off emotionally charged Iranians—this time, though, in a conflict of a quite different nature. At one point, thronging mourners upset the coffin, tumbling out the ayatollah's body. A helicopter had to be ordered down to lift it away from the melee.

The master of the Iranian revolution and the undisputed leader of its government was gone. His death left a huge void in Iranian society that would be virtually impossible to fill. Many Iranians had regarded Ayatollah Khomeini as an imam—not as one of the historic Twelve, but similar to them in stature as a spiritual leader. "Stern, demanding, and righteous, refusing to be seduced by materialism and power, Khomeini linked the Iranians to traditional faith and national identity," Mackey surmised. She added that the ayatollah "held a place in Iranian politics and culture that had never been occupied before nor is likely to be occupied by any other man again."[65]

9

Iran After Khomeini

The Pahlavis, father and son, dreamed of a return to grandeur for their country, harking back to the magnificence of ancient Persia. By the beginning of the twenty-first century, they hoped, it would be a model for the rest of the Middle East to follow. They even envisioned it as a world power.

What emerged instead is a nation that is neither a world power nor a model for the region. It little resembles the Persia of bygone splendor. In fact, some of its archaeological treasures were destroyed in the revolutionaries' zeal to forget the age of the dynasties.

But what of Ayatollah Khomeini's dream—the dream of a genuine Islamic state? It was Khomeini's dream that doomed the vision of the Pahlavis.

Iran's Council of Experts named Hojjatoleslam Ali Kahmanei to be *valayate-faqih*, Khomeini's successor in power and the ultimate leader of Iranian affairs. The *valayate-faqih* is appointed for life and has veto power over the decisions of the president and the Majlis. Kahmanei was president of Iran at the time of the ayatollah's death. The man originally selected to succeed Khomeini, Ayatollah Husein Ali Montazeri, had been dismissed shortly before Khomeini's death because he had expressed disagreements with the revolutionary regime. Hashemi Rafsanjani, speaker of the Majlis, became the new president.

The lifelong mission of Ayatollah Ruhollah Khomeini had been accomplished. The ulema, the men he insisted were best qualified to lead a government, were Iran's leaders. Historian Sandra Mackey wrote:

> In the most secular of ages he had raised the power of religion to assert Iran's Islamic identity. To a whole generation empowered by his revolutionary government, Khomeini had affirmed Islam as a way of life and had established the faith as a means of governing a modern society. For a people haunted by alien invasions, he had delivered the conviction that only through religion can Muslims end the humiliation and exploitation of their societies by the West.[66]

Some, however, have questioned just how much religion had to do with the Iranian Revolution or with its aftermath. "There is no doubt that the religious leaders, led by Khomeini, played an instrumental role in attacking the Shah's pro-Western, corrupt, and 'immoral' dictatorship," wrote Dr. Amin Saikal, a political scientist. "Their role, however, must not be overestimated, for the mass movements were not essentially religious. In fact, a large number of people who followed Khomeini were not necessarily practicing Muslims. Nor did they agree with Khomeini's idea of an Islamic Republic. They followed him because they shared a common opposition to the Shah's rule."[67]

In the 1994 book *Islam and the Post-Revolutionary State in Iran*, author Homa Omid declared, "Khomeini intended to build a thoroughly Islamic state, yet—despite the rhetoric—by the time he died, in terms of real politics Islam had become more of a posture than a reality."[68] Omid believed that because of the "conservatism of the religious institution . . . what has emerged over the past decade and a half is a stumbling, self-serving administration, that has failed its people and has chosen to forget the high-minded aims and ideals that Islam and Shiism had set."[69] The author concluded, "The first serious attempt at setting up an Islamic government in the twentieth century has proved to be an abysmal failure. In Iran all pretence of Islamification of the economy has been abandoned. Once more the country is turning to the West and attempting to borrow and perhaps spend its way out of its miseries."[70]

Regardless, the Shiite leadership—"political clerics," as they have been labeled[71]—remain in firm control over Iran. They have enjoyed relative freedom from a threat of military revolt, because Iran's military is quite divided. Its staunchly loyal Islamic Guard, a quarter-million strong, is as powerful as the regular army.

By the close of the century, however, most Iranians seemed to have decided the theocracy established by the 1979 revolution was not exactly what they wanted. The younger generation of Iranians craved a measure of freedom from the strict demands of Islamic hard-liners in everyday life. Young couples were weary of being chastised by frowning religious officials for holding hands while strolling down the street. Young women were pressing—privately, at least—for broader educational opportunities and relief from the laws and customs that gave men overbearing privileges. People of all ages and classes were tired of living in uncertainty and fear of what their government might do to them if they were even suspected of challenging the system. "We didn't expect so much austerity," one Iranian political commentator explained.[72] It's estimated that approximately a million Iranians left after the revolution, settling in the United States, Europe, and Canada.

Journalist and author Geneive Abdo, in her book *Answering Only to God*, described a 1994 press conference with President Rafsanjani:

> ... [A] brave young, female journalist asked if Iranian women could wear pink chadors and yellow head scarves in public. "Why do we always have to be cloaked in black? It is so depressing," she said. Rafsanjani replied that there was no religious edict requiring women to wear black. Bright colors would be a welcome change, he added. I was intrigued by his response, but Iranians explained later the president's assurances were in keeping with an entire tradition of telling people what they want to hear; everyone knew never to assume such comments would lead anywhere.[73]

Many of Iran's ruling Muslim clergy are what Mackey and other commentators termed "radicals" or "hard-liners."[74] "Portraying themselves as the champions of Islamic purity and the rights of the deprived," Mackey observed, "the hard-liners draw their following from the lower classes, the younger generation of clerical students, elements within the bureaucracy, and the all-important Revolutionary Guards."[75]

Other clerics might be described as "moderates" or "pragmatists." The difference between them and the hard-liners has little to do with religion beliefs—for they, too, are devout Shiites. Rather,

Mackey explained, it is the moderates' "recognition that Iran must live in the real world of economics and diplomacy. Forced to make a choice, they give priority to the nation rather than Islam."[76] Different Iranians support the moderates' ideas for different reasons. The moderate support base tends to lie in the middle class and those in business, as well as in much of the government bureaucracy.

In May 1997, voters overwhelmingly elected Muhammad Khatami president of their country to replace Rafsanjani. Khatami promised a more open society in which individuals' rights would be respected. Since then, the country has edged toward more liberal conditions. When Khatami traveled to Italy in March 1999, it marked the first time since the revolution that an Iranian leader had visited a Western nation. He was reelected in 2001. The constitution allows a president to serve only two terms.

Muslim fundamentalists, however, remain largely in charge of national affairs, including the military and the judicial system. And Islamic fundamentalism overshadows Iran. Abdo, a journalist who was based in Iran from 1998 to 2001, noted:

> The foreign visitor is struck by the startling absence of signs with directions to the next McDonald's or the next luxury hotel or advertisements for the latest in seductive designer jeans. Despite the odd sales pitch for a Japanese television here or a Korean mobile telephone there, most of the huge, painted billboards along the highways or the more simplistic sketches on downtown walls are selling the Islamic Revolution, the regime's single most valuable commodity.[77]

Islamic laws are rigidly enforced, and religious leaders pressure the people to adhere to traditional customs.

Full diplomatic relations between Iran and the United States never have been restored since the revolution. Iran maintains no embassy in the United States, and the United States has no official diplomatic delegation in Iran. As international terrorism heightened at the beginning of the new century, the administration of U.S. President George W. Bush cited Iran, Iraq, and

North Korea as the three major threats to American interests worldwide because of their weapons development programs and alleged support of terrorist organizations. The United States sent aid to Iran after a December 2003 earthquake killed more than thirty thousand people. The Tehran government, however, refused to allow Bush to dispatch a humanitarian delegation to the stricken area. It would have been the first formal visit by U.S. officials to Iran in more than 20 years.

Even though it attracts world attention less frequently or prominently than it did during the revolution, Iran still is perceived by many outsiders as a closed, intolerant, dangerous country. Fen Montaigne, writing for *National Geographic* magazine in 1999, explained that "change comes in fits and starts" as progressives in Iran struggle against unbending leadership. "Newspapers proliferate, exploring the limits of the allowable, and then are shut down. Reform politicians . . . are convicted on dubious corruption charges; five critics of the regime are mysteriously killed, and the government announces that rogue agents of the Intelligence Ministry have been arrested for the slayings.

"As the larger struggle has unfolded in Iran, many citizens have watched quietly, hoping Khatami and the reformers will prevail."[78]

Shiite leaders have at their disposal a secret police organization called the SAVAMA and a paramilitary Revolutionary Guard. They appoint the Muslim watchdog *komitehs* that observe activities in towns and communities, university campuses, and industrial workplaces. The komitehs, organized at the behest of Khomeini during the revolutionary period, demand strict adherence to Islam and the Islamic government. During the early 1980s, they established themselves as merciless persecutors of suspected troublemakers, and they executed countless individuals whom they considered enemies of the new republic. Today, they continue to monitor publications and broadcasting operations to see that all published statements are in line with the aims of the Revolutionary Council. Punishment is harsh for criticism of the government.

Basically, Iran since the revolution has functioned as the Shiite-controlled state Khomeini envisioned. To label it simply an

AYATOLLAH
RUHOLLAH
KHOMEINI

By becoming a Muslim religious teacher, Khomeini was following a long tradition, both in his own family and in his Iranian culture. Seen here in an ancient painting is Imam Shah Zaid preaching to his followers.

Seen here is the tomb of Fatima Ma'suma, located in the holy city of Qom. Fatimah was the sister of Ali al-Rida, one of the ancient imams. Her final resting place has long been a site to which devout Shiites have made pilgrimages.

As a young man, Khomeini became fiercely devoted to the Shiite form of Islam. He studied under many of the most prominent teachers of the day, and went on to become an influential teacher himself. This photograph was taken of Ruhollah Khomeini when he was twenty-five years old.

Although the shah of Iran intended to help his people by accepting the financial help and modern improvements gained through close relationships with the Western powers (and especially the United States), many traditional Muslims resented his attempts to secularize their society. The controversial Iranian shah and his wife are seen here in a 1970s photograph taken with U.S. President Jimmy Carter and First Lady Rosalynn Carter.

By 1979, Khomeini had been exiled, but opposition to the shah had become stronger than ever. Violent revolts, like that being led by the anti-shah protesters seen here, were almost a daily occurrence on the streets of Iran.

From his place of exile in France, Khomeini kept a close watch on events in his homeland, biding his time until he could return and capitalize on his popularity with fundamentalist Muslims.

Upon his return to Iran, the Ayatollah Khomeini took control over the nation. Beloved by the people, he was swarmed by followers who were eager to see and hear him firsthand everywhere he went.

Even after his death in 1989, Ayatollah Khomeini's legacy of radical fundamentalism in religion and politics has lived on in Iran—for good or for bad.

"Islamic fundamentalist" society, though, would be debatable. Muslims disagree among themselves as to what "fundamentalism" means, exactly. In his book *Islamic Fundamentalism: The New Global Threat*, Muhammad Mohaddessin asserted that Khomeini "was not a 'fundamentalist' who called for a return to the 'pure' Islam of the Prophet's time. What he preached and practiced was of his own making, far away from the Islam of Muhammad."[79] Mohaddessin, writing from his viewpoint as a leader of the People's Mojahedin, a political opposition group in Iran, pointed out: "The first thing Prophet Muhammad did when his army of Muslims conquered the city of Mecca in January A.D. 630 was to declare a general amnesty. The people of Mecca were free to choose or reject Islam."[80] The Qur'an, Mohaddessin noted, reiterates themes of compassion and mercy. This might seem in stark contrast to the bloody vendetta carried out by Khomeini's followers during and after the revolution.

Nevertheless, despite two decades of fighting, confusion, and the revolutionary regime's heavy hand, many Iranians have experienced notable improvements in their lives. As before the revolution, oil reserves continue to be Iran's chief economic resource. Iran is one of the world's leading oil exporters today. This has helped improve the quality of roads, utilities, and education, especially in rural locations.

Meanwhile, the people have enjoyed a gradual lifting of certain cultural restrictions. For example, journalist Robin Wright reported that by 1998, a surprising variety of popular American and European films were being screened in Iran: "American movies were no longer available only on the black market. They were also back in Iran's limited number of theaters and running on television."[81]

But Iranians face grave problems. These range from a weak economy to a shortage of usable water. Drug trafficking and abuse is rampant and growing, despite concerted efforts by the government to deter it (including a threatened death penalty for serious offenders). Because of its location, Iran is part of the illicit drug passageway between Southwest Asia and Europe.

In name and in principle, Ayatollah Ruhollah Khomeini was a religious—not political—leader. He became so extraordinarily popular and idolized, however, that extraordinary political change resulted from his spiritual teachings. Historians record that it was the religious nature of the movement that sets the revolution in Iran apart from those in America, France, and Russia.

Was the Iranian Revolution a success? Only in part, according to recent commentators. During the decades leading up to the revolution, Khomeini dreamed of a nation in which the "pure," strict law of Islam would be the basis of government and of all activity. When he came to power in the Islamic Republic of Iran, however, he soon found it would not work as envisioned. The Iranian people languished under government by repression. The people—the force who had brought the ayatollah to power—could not live under the type of rule Khomeini had demanded for so long. Substantial concessions had to be made. Meanwhile, other Islamic countries looked apprehensively at the effects of Khomeini's revolution.

Without question, the Iranian government sorely missed its revered leader. "When he died," wrote historian Sandra Mackey, "the Islamic Republic lost its all-important authority figure. In his absence, his heirs were left to struggle into the second decade of the revolution bleeding from their own divisions and bearing the burdens of the ayatollah's legacy."[82]

Elaine Sciolino, in her 2000 book *Persian Mirrors*, concluded:

> I've learned that it is impossible to talk about a monolithic Iranian "regime" any longer; the struggle for the country's future is far too intense for that. Today there is no unified leadership or all-powerful governmental superstructure that makes and executes all decisions. Rather, power is dispersed among and even within many competing power centers, with varying agendas and methods of operation and degrees of authority. Even as I write, alliances are shifting. Players are adapting. Coalitions are building.[83]

Whatever course Iran takes in coming years, Khomeini and his revolution brought changes that have affected not only Iran but the world. He forcefully brought Islam to the attention of millions of startled onlookers outside the Middle East. Until he came to power, most Westerners knew only that the Middle East was a region of vast oil resources, ageless history, and perpetual tension regarding Israel and the "Palestinian question." They little understood Islam or cared about its binding influence throughout society.

William Shawcross surmised, "Only with the rise of Khomeini did the politics and spirituality of Islam become a burning issue among strategists, conversationalists, politicians, and writers." [84]

c. 4000 B.C.   Settlements prospered in what is now Iran during the
Bronze Age

**Sixth to fifth
centuries B.C.**   Persia becomes a dominant Middle Eastern kingdom

**Early seventh
century A.D.**   Height of the Persian Empire

A.D. 622   Islam is established by the prophet Muhammad in what
is today Saudi Arabia and begins to spread across the
Middle East

632   Death of Muhammad; Islam soon becomes divided over
the line of succession, which will result in the Sunnite and
Shiite branches of the religion

c. 1902
Birth of
Ruhollah Khomeini

1941
Reza Shah Pahlavi is
succeeded by his son
Muhammad Reza

1900   1925   1950

c. 1920
Ruhollah goes to study under
Ayatollah Abdul Karim Haeri

1930
Ruhollah becomes a
Shiite teacher, takes the
1926   surname Khomeini
Reza Shah Pahlavi takes
control of independent Persia

680 An army of the caliph Yezid annihilates the much smaller force of Husain, a rival Islamic leader; Shiite Muslims today consider Husain a martyr, and the caliphs who succeeded Yezid pretenders to Islamic leadership

1501 Beginning of the Safavid Dynasty; the Shiite branch of Islam becomes the state religion of what is now Iran

1890–1892 The Tobacco Rebellion successfully challenges a British business interest in Persia

c. 1902 Birth of Ruhollah Khomeini

1903 Ruhollah's father is killed

1963
Khomeini and other religious leaders start riots against Pahlavi's "White Revolution"

1989
Death of Khomeini

1964
Khomeini is exiled

1980–1988
Iran-Iraq War

1960 **1975** **1990**

1977
Khomeini's son Mustafa dies mysteriously

1979
Shah Pahlavi leaves the country to the revolutionaries; Khomeini returns; Iran becomes an Islamic republic

CHRONOLOGY

1906 Religious leaders help force the ruling shah to accept a legislative governing body and a constitution; though short-lived, the arrangement signals effective opposition to the established government by Islamic influences

1908 Oil is discovered in the Khuzistan region of the country

1914 World War I begins; Russia and England establish presences in Persia

c. 1920 Ruhollah goes to Arak to study under Ayatollah Abdul Karim Haeri

1922 Haeri relocates to Qom, followed by Ruhollah and other students; Ruhollah in time becomes a teacher at the religious school in Qom

1926 After years of internal struggle and the ousting of foreign occupation forces, Reza Shah Pahlavi takes control of an independent Persia

1935 Pahlavi decrees that the former Persia will become known as Iran; he sets about to modernize the nation

1937 Ayatollah Haeri, Khomeini's mentor, dies; he will be replaced in 1944 by Ayatollah Muhammad Husayn Borujerdi

1941 Reza Shah Pahlavi is forced to abdicate; his twenty-one-year-old son, Muhammad Reza, succeeds him

1951–1953 Prime Minister Muhammad Mosaddiq threatens the authority of Muhammad Reza; after Reza briefly is frightened into fleeing the country, Mosaddiq is ousted and Reza is restored to power

1963 Khomeini and other religious leaders instigate riots against Pahlavi's "White Revolution"

1964 Khomeini goes to Turkey in exile; he relocates to Iraq the following year

1971 Shah Pahlavi's extravagant twenty-five-hundred-year Persian anniversary celebration at Persepolis brings renewed denunciations from the exiled Khomeini

1977 Khomeini's son Mustafa dies mysteriously

1978 The government's publicized opposition to Khomeini leads to demonstrations against the government; in the summer, protest leaders in Qom call for a general strike; demonstrations escalate into riots; in September, after the government bans demonstrations, throngs of protestors demand an end to the Pahlavi government and the return of Khomeini from exile; martial law is declared; when demonstrators gather in Tehran's Zhaleh Square on September 8 in defiance of the martial law curfew, armored units break up the gathering with heavy casualties; in October, Shah Pahlavi urges the government of Iraq to expel Khomeini; the ayatollah relocates to Paris, from where he accelerates his long-distance campaign against the shah; in December, students attack Western businesses and other targets; a curfew is declared, but with little effect; by mid-December, millions are demonstrating in Tehran; Shahpour Bakhtiar is appointed prime minister of Iran

1979 In January, Shah Pahlavi flies to Egypt, allegedly on vacation; at the command of Khomeini in Paris, an estimated million demonstrators turn out in Tehran to oppose Bakhtiar; on February 1, Khomeini returns to Tehran in triumph as protests explode into total revolution; by mid-month, Khomeini's radical followers effectively have overthrown the Iranian government; in April, Iran becomes an Islamic republic; in November, two weeks after the shah arrives in the United States for medical treatment, Iranians demanding his forced return swarm the U.S. Embassy in Tehran, taking fifty-two American hostages

CHRONOLOGY

1980 In January, Abolhassan Bani-Sadr is elected president of Iran; he hints at a solution to the heightening U.S. hostage crisis, but little progress is made; in April, President Jimmy Carter authorizes a secret military operation to attempt to free the American hostages; it ends in disastrous failure; in September, Iran is attacked by neighboring Iraq

1981 In January, the American hostages are released; in June, Bani-Sadr is ousted from office with Khomeini's consent

1988 A cease-fire is arranged in the Iran-Iraq War

1989 Khomeini orders the assassination of controversial author Salman Rushdie; on June 4, Khomeini dies

NOTES

CHAPTER 2:
THE "LAND BETWEEN EAST AND WEST"

1 Helen Chapin Metz, ed., *Iran: A Country Study*. Washington, D.C.: Federal Research Division, Library of Congress, 1989, p. 20.
2 Mohamed Heikal, *Iran: The Untold Story*. New York: Pantheon Books. 1982, p. 84.

CHAPTER 3:
THE SCHOLAR FROM KHOMEIN

3 Daniel Brumberg, *Reinventing Khomeini: The Struggle for Reform in Iran*. Chicago: The University of Chicago Press. 2001, p. 43.
4 Ibid., pp. 44–45.
5 Mohamed Heikal, *Iran: The Untold Story*. New York: Pantheon Books. 1982, p. 135.
6 Ibid.
7 Brumberg, p. 46.
8 Dilip Hiro, *Iran Under the Ayatollahs*. London, Boston, & Henley: Routledge & Kegan Paul, 1985, p. 50.
9 Roy Mottahedeh, *The Mantle of the Prophet: Religion and Politics in Iran*. New York: Simon & Schuster,1985, p. 187.
10 William Shawcross, *The Shah's Last Ride: The Fate of an Ally*. New York: Simon & Schuster, 1988, p. 113.
11 Ibid., p. 115.

CHAPTER 4:
SHAH PAHLAVI'S QUEST FOR GLORY

12 Lawrence Ziring, *The Middle East: A Political Dictionary*. Santa Barbara, CA: ABC-CLIO, Inc., 1992, p. 259.
13 Dilip Hiro, *Iran Under the Ayatollahs*. London, Boston, & Henley: Routledge & Kegan Paul, 1985, p. 2.
14 William Shawcross, *The Shah's Last Ride: The Fate of an Ally*. New York: Simon & Schuster, 1988, pp. 46–47.
15 Homa Omid, *Islam and the Post-Revolutionary State in Iran*. New York: St. Martin's Press, Inc., 1994, p. 34.
16 Sandra Mackey, *The Iranians: Persia, Islam and the Soul of a Nation*. New York: Penguin Group, 1996, p. 237.

CHAPTER 5:
SETTING THE STAGE FOR REVOLUTION

17 Dilip Hiro, *Iran Under the Ayatollahs*. London, Boston, & Henley: Routledge & Kegan Paul, 1985, p. 51.
18 Roy Mottahedeh, *The Mantle of the Prophet: Religion and Politics in Iran*. New York: Simon & Schuster,1985, p. 242.
19 Nikki R. Keddie, *Roots of Revolution: An Interpretive History of Modern Iran*. New Haven & London: Yale University Press, 1981, p. 205.
20 Matthew Gordon, *Ayatollah Khomeini*. Philadelphia: Chelsea House Publishers, 1988, pp. 60–61.
21 Mottahedeh, pp. 191–192.
22 Akbar Husain, *The Revolution in Iran*. Vero Beach, FL: Rourke Enterprises, Inc., 1988, p. 26.
23 Sandra Mackey, *The Iranians: Persia, Islam and the Soul of a Nation*. New York: Penguin Group, 1996, p. 274.

CHAPTER 6:
THE SHAH'S GOVERNMENT COLLAPSES

24 Mohamed Heikal, *Iran: The Untold Story*. New York: Pantheon Books. 1982, p. 95.
25 Matthew Gordon, *Ayatollah Khomeini*. Philadelphia: Chelsea House Publishers, 1988, p. 87.
26 Elaine Sciolino, *Persian Mirrors: The Elusive Face of Iran*. New York: The Free Press, 2000, p. 49.
27 Amin Saikal, *The Rise and Fall of the Shah*. Princeton, NJ: Princeton University Press, 1980, p. 4.
28 William Shawcross, *The Shah's Last Ride: The Fate of an Ally*. New York: Simon & Schuster, 1988, pp. 20–21.
29 Ibid., p. 35.
30 Akbar Husain, *The Revolution in Iran*. Vero Beach, FL: Rourke Enterprises, Inc., 1988, p. 9.
31 Ibid., p. 10.
32 Roy Mottahedeh, *The Mantle of the Prophet: Religion and Politics in Iran*. New York: Simon & Schuster,1985, p. 377.

NOTES

CHAPTER 7:
KHOMEINI IN POWER

33 Dilip Hiro, *Iran Under the Ayatollahs.* London, Boston, & Henley: Routledge & Kegan Paul, 1985, p. 263.

34 William Shawcross, *The Shah's Last Ride: The Fate of an Ally.* New York: Simon & Schuster, 1988, pp. 199–200.

35 Akbar Husain, *The Revolution in Iran.* Vero Beach, FL: Rourke Enterprises, Inc., 1988, p. 49.

36 Elaine Sciolino, *Persian Mirrors: The Elusive Face of Iran.* New York: The Free Press, 2000, p. 51.

37 Elton L. Daniel, *The History of Iran.* Westport, CT: Greenwood Press, 2001, p. 15.

38 Robin Wright, *The Last Great Revolution: Turmoil and Transformation in Iran.* New York: Alfred A. Knopf, 2000, pp. xii, xiii.

39 Matthew Gordon, *Ayatollah Khomeini.* Philadelphia: Chelsea House Publishers, 1988, p. 93.

40 Ibid., p. 73.

41 James Haskins, *Leaders of the Middle East.* Hillside, NJ: Enslow Publishers, Inc., 1985, p. 119.

42 Lawrence Ziring, *The Middle East: A Political Dictionary.* Santa Barbara, CA: ABC-CLIO, Inc., 1992, p. 152.

43 Said Amir Arjomand, *The Turban for the Crown: The Islamic Revolution in Iran.* New York and Oxford: Oxford University Press, 1988, p. 154.

44 Haskins, p. 122.

45 Ibid.

CHAPTER 8:
A TROUBLED DECADE

46 Elaine Sciolino, *Persian Mirrors: The Elusive Face of Iran.* New York: The Free Press, 2000, p. 51.

47 Daniel Brumberg, *Reinventing Khomeini: The Struggle for Reform in Iran.* Chicago: The University of Chicago Press. 2001, p. 98.

48 Ibid.

49 Nikki R. Keddie, *Roots of Revolution: An Interpretive History of Modern Iran.* New Haven & London: Yale University Press, 1981, p. 267.

50 Mohamed Heikal, *Iran: The Untold Story.* New York: Pantheon Books. 1982, p. 136.

51 Dilip Hiro, *Iran Under the Ayatollahs.* London, Boston, & Henley: Routledge & Kegan Paul, 1985, p. 264.

52 Sandra Mackey, *The Iranians: Persia, Islam and the Soul of a Nation.* New York: Penguin Group, 1996, p. 335.

53 Ibid., p. 336.

54 Roy Mottahedeh, *The Mantle of the Prophet: Religion and Politics in Iran.* New York: Simon & Schuster,1985, p. 9.

55 Heikal, pp. 184–185.

56 Matthew Gordon, *Ayatollah Khomeini.* Philadelphia: Chelsea House Publishers, 1988, p. 105.

57 Heikal, p. 87.

58 James Haskins, *Leaders of the Middle East.* Hillside, NJ: Enslow Publishers, Inc., 1985, p. 121.

59 William L. Cleveland, *A History of the Modern Middle East.* Boulder, CO: Westview Press, 1994, p. 398.

60 From an advertisement reproduced in Gordon, p. 99.

61 Elton L. Daniel, *The History of Iran.* Westport, CT: Greenwood Press, 2001, p. 227.

62 Ibid.

63 Mackey, p. 334.

64 Geneive Abdo and Jonathan Lyons, *Answering Only to God: Faith and Freedom in Twenty-First-Century Iran.* New York: Henry Holt and Company, LLC., 2003, p. 284.

65 Mackey, p. 346.

CHAPTER 9: IRAN AFTER
KHOMEINI

66 Sandra Mackey, *The Iranians: Persia, Islam and the Soul of a Nation.* New York: Penguin Group, 1996, p. 355.

67 Amin Saikal, *The Rise and Fall of the Shah.* Princeton, NJ: Princeton University Press, 1980, p. 204.

68 Homa Omid, *Islam and the Post-Revolutionary State in Iran.* New York: St. Martin's Press, Inc., 1994, p. 153.

69 Ibid., p. 1.

70 Ibid., p. 219.

71 Mackey, p. 355.

72 Don Belt, ed., *The World of Islam.* Washington, D.C.: National Geographic Society, 2001, p. 241.

73 Geneive Abdo and Jonathan Lyons, *Answering Only to God: Faith and Freedom in Twenty-First-Century Iran.* New York: Henry Holt and Company, LLC., 2003, pp. 216–217.

74 Mackey, p. 343.

75 Ibid., p. 344.

76 Ibid., p. 345.

77 Abdo and Lyons, p. 258.

78 Belt, p. 241.

79 Mohammad Mohaddessin, *Islamic Fundamentalism: The New Global Threat.*

Washington, D.C.: Seven Locks Press, 1993, p. xxiii.

80 Ibid., p. 3.

81 Robin Wright, *The Last Great Revolution: Turmoil and Transformation in Iran.* New York: Alfred A. Knopf, 2000, p. 131.

82 Mackey, p. 335.

83 Elaine Sciolino, *Persian Mirrors: The Elusive Face of Iran.* New York: The Free Press, 2000, p. 360.

84 William Shawcross, *The Shah's Last Ride: The Fate of an Ally.* New York: Simon & Schuster, 1988, p. 110.

BIBLIOGRAPHY

Abdo, Geneive, and Jonathan Lyons. *Answering Only to God: Faith and Freedom in Twenty-First-Century Iran.* Henry Holt and Company, LLC, 2003.

Arjomand, Said Amir. *The Turban for the Crown: The Islamic Revolution in Iran.* Oxford University Press, 1988.

Belt, Don, ed. *The World of Islam.* National Geographic Society, 2001.

Brumberg, Daniel. *Reinventing Khomeini: The Struggle for Reform in Iran.* The University of Chicago Press, 2001.

Cleveland, William L. *A History of the Modern Middle East.* Westview Press, 1994.

Daniel, Elton L. *The History of Iran.* Greenwood Press, 2001.

Gordon, Matthew. *Ayatollah Khomeini.* Chelsea House Publishers, 1988.

Haskins, James. *Leaders of the Middle East.* Enslow Publishers, Inc., 1985.

Hawkes, Jacquetta. *The First Great Civilizations: Life in Mesopotamia, the Indus Valley, and Egypt.* Alfred A. Knopf, 1973.

Heikal, Mohamed. *Iran: The Untold Story.* Pantheon Books, 1982.

Hiro, Dilip. *Iran Under the Ayatollahs.* Routledge & Kegan Paul, 1985.

Husain, Akbar. *The Revolution in Iran.* Rourke Enterprises, Inc., 1988.

Keddie, Nikki R. *Roots of Revolution: An Interpretive History of Modern Iran.* Yale University Press, 1981.

Mackey, Sandra. *The Iranians: Persia, Islam and the Soul of a Nation.* Penguin Group, 1996.

Metz, Helen Chapin, ed. *Iran: A Country Study.* Federal Research Division, Library of Congress, 1989.

The Middle East, 9th ed. CQ Press, A Division of Congressional Quarterly Inc., 2000.

Mohaddessin, Mohammad. *Islamic Fundamentalism: The New Global Threat*. Seven Locks Press,1993.

Mottahedeh, Roy. *The Mantle of the Prophet: Religion and Politics in Iran*. Simon & Schuster, 1985.

Omid, Homa. *Islam and the Post-Revolutionary State in Iran*. St. Martin's Press, Inc., 1994.

Saikal, Amin. The *Rise and Fall of the Shah*. Princeton University Press, 1980.

Sciolino, Elaine. *Persian Mirrors: The Elusive Face of Iran*. The Free Press, 2000.

Shawcross, William. *The Shah's Last Ride: The Fate of an Ally*. Simon & Schuster, 1988.

Wright, Robin. *The Last Great Revolution: Turmoil and Transformation in Iran*. Alfred A. Knopf, 2000.

Ziring, Lawrence. *The Middle East: A Political Dictionary*. ABC-CLIO, Inc., 1992.

INTERNET SOURCES

"Iran's Century of Upheaval," BBC News.
news.bbc.co.uk/1/hi/world/middle_east/618649.stm

The *World Factbook*, maintained by the
U.S. Central Intelligence Agency.
www.cia.gov/cia/publications/factbook/geos/ir.html

FURTHER READING

PRIMARY SOURCES

Algar, Hamid. *Roots of the Islamic Revolution in Iran (Four Lectures)*. Islamic Publications International, 2001.

Khomeini, Ayatollah Ruhollah. *Islam and Revolution I: Writings and Declarations of Imam Khomeini (1941–1980)*, trans. Hamid Algar. Mizan Press, 1981.

———. *The Sayings of Ayatollah Khomeini*. Bantam Books, 1985.

SECONDARY SOURCES

Alden, Carella. *Royal Persia: Tales and Art of Iran*. Parents' Magazine Press, 1972.

Belt, Don, ed. *The World of Islam*. National Geographic Society, 2001.

Daniel, Elton L. *The History of Iran*. Greenwood Press, 2001.

Gordon, Matthew. *Ayatollah Khomeini*. Chelsea House Publishers, 1988.

Greenblatt, Miriam. *Iran*. Children's Press, 2003.

Kheirabadi, Masoud. *Iran*. Chelsea House Publishers, 2003.

———. *Islam*. Chelsea House Publishers, 2004.

Wagner, Heather Lehr. *Iran*. Chelsea House Publishers, 2003.

WEBSITES

Iran Chamber Society

http://www.iranchamber.com/history/rkhomeini/ayatollah_khomeini.php

This site presents a thorough history of the Iranian Revolution and the life and career of Ayatollah Khomeini.

Iranian Cultural Information Center

http://www.persia.org/

Provides detailed information about Iran's history, religion and politics, and current affairs.

Khomeini.com

http://www.khomeini.com/

This site, which includes biographical, historical, and religious information as well as documents from Khomeini's life, provides an admiring view of his career and impact.

NetIran

http://www.netiran.com/

Provides a broad glimpse of life in Iran, from lists of political leaders to profiles of historical and cultural happenings.

The Story of the Revolution

http://www.bbc.co.uk/persian/revolution/rev_01.shtml

Part of the site of the British Broadcasting Corporation (BBC), this page traces the history of the Iranian Revolution and includes interesting documents about the major players, including Ayatollah Khomeini.

The Time 100: The Most Important People of the Century

http://www.time.com/time/time100/leaders/profile/khomeini.html

Provides a profile of Khomeini and his dramatic impact on the history of Iran, the Islamic faith, and the world.

GLOSSARY

ayatollah—The highest-ranking category of Shiite clerics; the word means "sign of God."

caliph—Ruler of historic Persia and spiritual leader of Sunnite Islam.

Caucasus—The territory situated north of northwestern Iran, between the Black Sea and Caspian Sea.

doshak—Blanket.

faqih—Islamic legal scholar.

hojatalislam—The category of Shiite teacher just below the level of ayatollah.

imam—Traditionally, one of the twelve select leaders who, according to Shiite tradition, have been ordained by God to interpret Qur'anic teachings; the twelfth, or "hidden," imam vanished more than a thousand years ago, Shiites believe, but lingers in spirit and someday is coming to bring justice to the world.

jihad—An Islamic holy war; literally, a war to establish God's law.

komiteh—One of thousands of "revolutionary committees" formed to monitor life in post-revolutionary Iran.

madreseh—An Islamic school.

Majlis—Iran's elected parliament.

mullah—A Muslim religious leader in a community.

mustazafin—The poor class in Iran.

nationalize—To bring an industry under national or government control.

Qur'an—The holy book of the Islamic religion.

shah—Ruler or "king of kings" of Persia.

ulema—Shiite teachers.

INDEX

INDEX

in United States for medical treatment, 62
and United States support, 29–30, 40
and "White Revolution," 30, 37–38
and Yezid, 12
Pahlavi, Reza Shah, 14–16
and abdication, 16
and Iran as name for Persia, 15
Khomeini's contempt for, 24–25, 36
and modernization of Iran, 14–16, 25, 82
as shah, 14
Pahlavi Dynasty, 14.
See also Pahlavi, Muhammad Reza; Pahlavi, Reza Shah
painting, and Islamic Republic of Iran, 72
Palestine Liberation Organization (PLO), 57, 77
Paris, Khomeini exiled to, 50–51, 63
peasants, and Islamic Republic of Iran, 69
People's Mojahedin, 87
Persepolis ("City of Persia")
Darius establishing, 7
and twenty-five-hundred-year Persian anniversary celebration, 31–32
Persia, 7–15
and Arab invaders, 9–12
early settlements in, 7
and Empire, 7–12
and Great Britain, 12, 13, 14
as "land between East and West," 7
and legislature and constitution, 14
and meaning of, 15
and oil, 14
and Qajar Dynasty, 12–14, 20
and religion, 9, 12. *See also* Islam
and Russia, 12, 14
and Safavid Dynasty, 12
and Turkey, 12, 14
and twenty-five-hundred-year Persian anniversary celebration, 31–32

and *ulema*, 12–14, 15–16
and World War I, 14.
See also Pahlavi, Muhammad Reza; Pahlavi, Reza Shah
Plato, 22
poison gas, and Hussein, 73
political parties, 29, 45, 45–46, 57, 58, 66
and Islamic Republic of Iran, 63, 65–66
Pompidou, Georges, 31
poverty
Khomeini on, 24–25, 37, 39, 70
and Muhammad Reza Pahlavi, 30, 32
and oil, 28
prose, and Islamic Republic of Iran, 72
prostitutes, and Islamic Republic of Iran, 60

Qajar, Aga Muhammad, 12
Qajar Dynasty, 12–14, 20
Qom, 21–24
and Iranian Revolution, 37–39
Khomeini as teacher in, 19, 21, 22, 24–25, 35, 36–37, 41
Khomeini meeting public in after Revolution, 57
Khomeini studying in, 21–22, 24
Khomeini's headquarters in, 74–75
Khomeini's writings in, 36–37
and Madraseh Faizieh, 21, 23, 24, 37, 38–39
protests against Muhammad Reza Pahlavi in, 47
and tomb of Fatimah Ma'suma, 14, 21
Qotbzadeh, Sadiq, 66
and conspiracy plot, 77
quality of life, and Islamic Republic of Iran, 87
Qur'an (Koran), 11, 20, 22, 24, 78–79, 87

Rafsanjani, Hashemi, 82, 84, 85
Rajai, Muhammad Ali, 63

INDEX

ABOUT THE CONTRIBUTORS

DANIEL E. HARMON (*www.danieleltonharmon.com*) is an author and editor in Spartanburg, South Carolina. He has written some forty non-fiction books, one historical mystery short story collection, and numerous magazine and newspaper articles. Harmon has served for many years as editor of *The Hornpipe*, an online folk music project (*www.hornpipe.com*); associate editor of *Sandlapper: The Magazine of South Carolina*; and editor of *The Lawyer's PC*, a national computer newsletter published by West.

MARTIN E. MARTY is an ordained minister in the Evangelical Lutheran Church and the Fairfax M. Cone Distinguished Service Professor Emeritus at the University of Chicago Divinity School, where he taught for thirty-five years. Marty has served as president of the American Academy of Religion, the American Society of Church History, and the American Catholic Historical Association, and was also a member of two U.S. presidential commissions. He is currently Senior Regent at St. Olaf College in Northfield, Minnesota. Marty has written more than fifty books, including the three-volume *Modern American Religion* (University of Chicago Press). His book *Righteous Empire* was a recipient of the National Book Award.